D0867641

"*Bridging the Value Gap* is a practical gu[...]
consultative approach that affluent client[...]
provides a powerful client-focused framework that will help
any financial advisor take their practice to the next level."

**BARRY ROCHLIN**
*Financial Advisor*
*20-year Veteran Merrill Lynch*

▲

"In the prescription-driven, product-pushing, one-size-fits-all
marketing environment financial advisors and consumers alike
must now navigate, Rieman redirects our focus and redefines
our role in this challenging and ever-changing environment.
Rieman effectively teaches us how to rise to that next level of client
relations and demonstrates how to operate a client-led practice
so we as advisors are strategically positioned as the genuine
champions and guardians of our clients' estate."

**ANDREW MILLER**
*Retirement Planning Specialist*
*AXA Equitable*

▲

"Finally, a blueprint for advisors, wholesalers and
other professionals in our industry that can help us
truly serve our clients."

**BRYCE JOHNSON**
*National Sales Manager*
*Cambridge Petroleum Group*

▲

"This book is a great reminder that a client first approach leads
to great business results and it's a no-nonsense refresher on
how to do it – *Bridging the Value Gap* is a must read."

**MYLES MORIN**
*SVP Wealth Management*
*Manulife Financial*

▲

"*Bridging the Value Gap* is a book you'll
come back to time and time again"

**MIKE SHIELDS**
*Financial Advisor*
*Global Wealth Management Morgan Stanley*

## FROM THE AUTHOR, *October 2008*

I wrote *Bridging the Value Gap* because from my vantage point as an industry professional and as an industry consumer the need for more client-focused advisors was unmistakable. It was obvious to me, and many I spoke with, that the needs of the consumer had evolved well beyond the offerings and approach of most in the financial services industry. While I was sure that change would occur, driven by consumer demand, I assumed it would be gradual and like turning a big ship it would take time. Instead the world financial crises in the fall of 2008 accelerated this change and the need for financial advisors to embrace a more client-focused business model. Advisors that don't align their practice with what consumers demand are clearly in danger of becoming irrelevant and firms that don't will continue to experience the flight of affluent assets.

The insights and concepts within *Bridging the Value Gap* are even more important for the success and sustainability of your practice as a result of the financial crisis in 2008. The events fundamentally changed the world of the financial services industry. The change was swift and dramatic with serious ramifications for most financial advisors. Over a three-week period consumer trust in our industry all but evaporated. A Prince & Associates study (Rich Investors Blame Advisors, *Wall Street Journal*, Oct. 4-5, 2008) found that, as a result of the financial meltdown, 81% of investors with $1 million or more of investible assets planned to take money away from their current advisor. Yet even worse, 86% of affluent clients planned to tell other investors to avoid their advisor. This number became even more pronounced for brand name firms with 90% of their clients saying they would take money away from the firm. Yet only 2% of affluent clients surveyed said they would recommend their advisor and firm to other investors, bleak numbers indeed.

Clearly the affluent market will only work with financial advisors they deem to be true advisors. Are you that advisor? If not, the time to change is now.

# Bridging the Value Gap:

A Financial Advisor's
Guide to Being a
True Advisor and
Attracting More
Affluent Clients

## Thomas F. Rieman

With Commentary from Top Financial Advisor

Robert L. Schein

## To my Parents

*for instilling in me a deep passion
for reading and science*

## To Kathy

*for her love and support*

# Table of Contents

Chapter 4:

Chapter 5:

Chapter 6:

**Table of Contents** *Continued*

# Acknowledgements

This book would not have been possible without the influence and help of many people. To begin I'm so very thankful to my parents for instilling in me the love of reading and the thirst for knowledge. To my mother for surrounding me with books since as far back as I can remember and to my father for passing on a real love of science.

I'm indebted to the clients I've worked with over the last two decades. It's through my work with them that I've gained a truly intimate understanding of the financial services industry and conceived the practices found in this book. My thanks to Myles Morin and Paul Swanson for trusting me early on and to Jim Fitzpatrick, CFP (aka Fitz) for what I learned in our many hours of teaching together.

I owe much to the faculty and my fellow inaugural cohort at George Mason University's Program for Social and Organizational Learning (now the Program for Organizational Development and Knowledge Management), to Don Lavoie *(in memory of)*, Tojo Thatchenkery, Mark Addleson and Ann Baker for helping me see the world in a whole new way and whose teachings are the very foundation of this book.

I'm also grateful to Mary Malyszka and Bryce Johnson for their timely and insightful editing and to Tim Ravenna for his tireless efforts in designing the book. And of course my sincere appreciation to Robert Schein for the many phone calls and his invaluable input and participation.

Finally, I'm very thankful for my wife Kathy and her love, support and patience during the lengthy and often all consuming task of writing this book.

# The Financial Advisor's Responsible Opportunity

> *"Know the truth so to change the heart, change the heart in order to change attitudes, change attitudes in order to change the course of life. This is producing the good life, a life of significance, relevance and beauty."*
>
> *–Stuart Briscoe*

As a financial advisor you have a significant responsibility. The outcome of the "advice" you give can mean the difference between someone realizing their ideal life or living a life where choice and even dignity are lost. At the same time today's affluent market - from the mass affluent to the very affluent - presents an unprecedented opportunity as the need for sound financial guidance is at an all time high. And it is the few financial advisors that best fulfill their responsibility, the advisors that provide the comprehensive and consultative services today's affluent consumers want and need, that are experiencing the greatest success.

So to help you better fulfill the role of "true advisor" and as a consequence attract more affluent clients, *Bridging the Value Gap* offers a guide to replicating the practices employed by the most successful advisors in the industry. It provides a framework – *The Seven Practices* - to assist you, whether you're new to the business, a seasoned veteran or somewhere in between, in further aligning you're practice with the needs of the affluent market. Using this book as an ongoing reference guide will help you integrate the perspectives, knowledge, language and processes proven to drive practice success.

Ultimately the goal of *Bridging the Value Gap* is to help you see the importance of embracing a client-focused business model, to change your attitude as to your purpose and role as a financial advisor, to change the course of your business and ultimately to help you lead a life of greater significance and relevance – to help you become a true advisor and produce the good life, for you and those you serve.

## THE SEVEN PRACTICES
of High-Value Financial Services Professionals-

THE PATH TO HIGHER PERFORMANCE

# THE NEED

Navigating a highly volatile world, facing financial uncertainty, and understanding the complexity of "financial planning" are daunting tasks for most. Without professional advice and direction many are in danger of not living the life they hoped for. This is why skillful financial advisors are so important; to provide the advice consumers need to realize their ideal future and to get the most life out of their money.

"Advise", by definition means to counsel and provide guidance. And today's consumer is looking for just that; sound and sage advice to help them realize their financial and life goals. Yet accepting guidance is based on the willingness to be guided; it's based on your client's trust in you. Do you have the trust of your clients to guide them past the constant noise generated by the twenty four-hour news stations micro analyzing the market and the ubiquitous street corner advice, or are you forced to respond to the panic, greed and confusion that emersion in it creates? What do you do in times when even well constructed portfolios aren't immune to market dynamics and asset allocation "doesn't work"? You have a process that works in up, down and sideways markets, right? Well at least you have the "relationship" to fall back on. You do, don't you?

# THE VALUE GAP

Unfortunately research reveals that this is not the case for a majority of financial advisors. Most advisors have neither a process that is bulletproof in all markets, nor the depth of relationships needed to effectively lead clients past the noise and emotion to achieve the outcomes they desire. Instead many advisors employ decidedly industry-centric, product-focused practices that not only fall short of satisfying consumer needs, but also repel the very clients they want to attract.

There is a fundamental disconnect between the product-focused practices so prevalent in the financial services industry and the needs of today's consumer, particularly the affluent. Competitive convergence has removed all but the subtlest in differences in products and the mass proliferation of product, the "arms race" in the financial services industry, has not translated into a better consumer experience, in fact quite the opposite.

For many advisors attracting better clients requires more than just incremental improvement. Instead it requires a fundamentally new business model, a business model focused on value not product; one that provides a framework for offering the comprehensive services and consultative approach consumers demand and deserve.

Numerous books have been written for financial advisors about working in the "affluent" marketplace and they generally focus on what an <u>advisor needs to do</u> to pursue the affluent market. *Bridging the Value Gap* is different as it focuses on what an <u>advisor needs to be</u> to attract more affluent clients.

This book offers robust guidance and instruction on building a higher value, higher performance advisory practice through *The Seven Practices of High-Value Financial Services Professionals*[TM] – a business model representative of what the best in the industry do. *The Seven Practices* offer the framework, knowledge, language, and key processes to help you fully align your role, your offerings and your approach with the needs of today's consumer and be the trusted advisor they're looking for – to help you attract better and more clients and build a more successful and sustainable practice.

*Bridging the Value Gap* is Divided Into Five Sections

SECTION ONE presents a business case for change in the financial services industry, exploring the need to elevate the practices of today's financial advisors and offering a client-focused business model as a method to do so.

SECTION TWO provides insight and guidance on employing Practice 1 & 2, a client first strategy and a deep understanding of the value you can offer — the foundational practices of the most successful financial advisors in the industry.

SECTION THREE explores Practices 3 & 4 and how the best begin to deliver on their client-focused strategy by offering the comprehensive services that affluent consumers are demanding.

SECTION FOUR delves in to Practice 5, the high performance business processes – advanced strategic planning, branding, marketing, innovation, partnering, and metrics – that enable top advisors to maximize their market impact.

---

Finally, SECTION FIVE looks at Practices 6 & 7, the ability to convey real value and to employ a highly consultative client-focused advisory process, the crowning practices of the most successful financial advisors in the industry.

---

At the end of each section you'll find *The Seven Practices Toolkit*. The toolkit provides guidance and instruction on integrating each of *The Seven Practices* to help you make the change, whether transformational or incremental, needed to be a true advisor.

## MOVING FORWARD

I wrote this book with Robert's collaboration because we believe deeply in the need for change in the financial services industry, financial advisors and the wholesalers that support them. The ultimate purpose of *Bridging the Value Gap*, the theories, framework, language and processes within, along with Robert's insight and commentary, is to help financial advisors institute positive change and become the true advisors that affluent consumers want to work with.

*Bridging the Value Gap* is a reference book – an instructional guide – so use it accordingly. Read it. Refer to it often. Highlight it. Make notes in it. Build a support network. Use resources within your broker dealer or firm and leverage your wholesalers. Use them as sounding boards, coaches, and sponsors. But most of all make the decision to change – make the decision to be a true advisor to your clients and set yourself apart from the many to being one of the few.

You won't regret it. In fact, it may be the most important thing you'll ever do as a financial advisor.

Tom Rieman

*Founder, Impact Training and Consulting*
*Parker, Texas*

*Bridging the Value Gap*

# A Note from Robert Schein

In early 2008 I was part of a panel for an industry conference that discussed what it means to be a "trusted advisor". Tom was in the audience and afterwards, by chance, we met. He introduced himself, said he enjoyed my comments, and shared that he was writing a book on the practices of the best financial advisors. Tom said he was interested in my perspective and asked if we could continue our conversation after the conference. I agreed.

We talked a few weeks later, Tom laid out the concepts and ideas of his "book project" and it soon became readily apparent to me that we have much in common in our view of what it means be a great financial advisor. So when Tom asked if I was interested in collaborating by providing commentary to add additional perspective to the concepts in the book, I responded with an enthusiastic "yes".

I thought it would be a great partnership. I was right. The more we worked together, and as I watched the concepts and ideas emerge on paper, the more I realized how important this book is and how valuable it will be in the hands of serious financial advisors.

*Bridging the Value Gap* is a roadmap to building the kind of practice that sets advisors apart, attracts great clients and keeps them for life. I am fortunate to have made the decision early in my career to go down the path the concepts in this book represent and because of that decision, today, our team manages over $400 million in assets.

A powerful tool for any advisor whether new to the business or an established veteran, this book can change your life and the life of your clients. Integrating the practices found in this book will help you build an even more successful and even more robust practice and, at the same time, help your clients realize the success they desire, demand, and deserve.

So use the concepts and ideas in the following pages to make a better life for you and your clients.

Robert Schein
*Wealth Advisor, Morgan Stanley*
*Palm Desert, California*

# A Word to the Financial Services Wholesaler

While the primary audience of this book is the financial advisor, *Bridging the Value Gap* is also for you, the wholesaler. It's a guide to help you deliver the support that today's advisors want and need and a framework to build more productive and loyal advisor relationships. Whether you're a seasoned pro or new to the field this book will help you further align your practice with what corner office producers want and emerging advisors need. The ideas and concepts found in the following chapters will help you deliver the value added services that transcend product and meet the standards of top producers while supporting emerging advisors in taking their practice to the next level.

*Bridging the Value Gap* provides the framework, processes and language to help you have an even greater impact on the success of the advisors you work with, to play an integral role in helping them employ the comprehensive and consultative services proven to drive top producer success.

## HOW TO USE THIS BOOK

First use it to improve your own practice. This starts with reading the book, learning from what it has to offer and striving to master the practices within it. The ideas and concepts discussed in the following pages are just as applicable to you as the financial advisor and will help you become an even better resource for the advisors in your territory, to be the wholesaler that even the very best advisors value. Once you have a grasp of the concepts you can use *Bridging the Value Gap* as a tool to help advisors grow their business. Introduce the book and coach to the concepts within it. Use it as an explicit guide to assist advisors in employing the comprehensive and consultative services proven to attract the more affluent client.

Ultimately, *Bridging the Value Gap* will help you be a true strategic partner to the advisors you work with and be of value time and time again.

# The Opportunity

**SECTION ONE** presents a business case for change in the financial services industry; it explores the need to elevate the practices of today's financial advisors and offers a client-focused business model as a method to do so.

**CHAPTER ONE** *The Death of a Business Model* explores the disconnects between the needs of today's consumers and the product-focused practices of most advisors along with the dangers this value-gap presents to practice success and sustainability.

In response to this value-gap, **CHAPTER TWO**, *The Seven Practices of High-Value Financial Services Professionals*, presents a value and client-focused business model, representative of what the best in the industry do, as a framework to help advisors employ the practices affluent consumers are actively seeking.

SECTION

1

# The Death of a Business Model

Globally the number of affluent and emerging affluent individuals and families is growing. In North America alone there are more than twenty-one million affluent consumers with over $76 trillion in assets. We are entering a time of unprecedented opportunity for financial advisors, as many of these consumers want financial advice and are seeking professional help. Yet most advisors are being left out. Clients and their money are flowing to a relatively few and correspondingly very successful financial advisors. Why is this so? What is keeping so many advisors and maybe even you from attracting more affluent clients and building a million dollar practice?

> *"Standing still is the fastest way of moving backwards in a rapidly changing world"*
> *–Lauren Bacall*

The reason for this disparity is twofold:

1. **The value gap** A shift in consumer needs has rendered the business models and sales practices of the majority of advisors far less effective.

2. **Competitive convergence and strategic decay** Both have greatly diminished an advisors ability to create real sustainable advantages and stand out in a crowded and competitive market.

## THE VALUE GAP

The needs of the consuming public are changing; the issues they face are more complex and the outcome of their financial decisions even more important. As a result the product and investment-focused business models and sales practices employed by the majority of advisors no longer fully satisfy the needs of today's consuming public. There are distinct disconnects – a fundamental value gap – between the wants and needs of today's consumer and the offerings and approach of most advisors.

These disconnects arise in the following areas.

## FOCUS

While consumers are focused on their own financial goals and what they need to do maximize their success product-focused advisors tend to focus on their own specialty/product niche and what they need to do to sell more.

## OBJECTIVE

The consumer's objective is to achieve their goals as efficiently and effectively as possible, yet the product-focused advisor's primary objective is to sell product.

## EXPERTISE

Consumers need advisors with real breadth and depth of knowledge and an expertise that transcends product mastery to help them get the most from their wealth and realize their ideal life. However the knowledge and expertise of product-focused advisors is generally limited to depth in their product niche.

## DELIVERABLES

Consumers need comprehensive services and advice to navigate the myriad of impediments that can keep them from realizing their goals. Yet product-focused advisors offerings and advice are generally limited to their product or investment specialty.

## COMMUNICATION

Consumers want to gain a better and more thorough understanding of the complex issues they face and strategic options they have to choose from. Unfortunately product-focused advisors regularly communicate in industry jargon and technical terms that often mean little to consumers.

## PROCESS

Consumers want to work in a collaborative and consultative relationship; they want a strategic partner to help them realize their goals. But the transactional approach of product-focused advisors is more about the sales call, the pitch, and closing the business.

## ROLE

Ultimately consumers are looking for a true advisor; someone who is truly focused on and capable of helping them realize their very intimate and important life goals. Yet, product-focused advisors are fundamentally salespeople and primarily focused on their own success.

| THE DISCONNECTS | Product-Focused Business Model Attributes | Consumer Needs |
|---|---|---|
| Focus | Product Niche | Their Own Issues and Goals |
| Objective | Sell Product | Achieve Financial Goals & Realize Ideal Life |
| Expertise | Narrow and Deep Product Specific | Broad and Deep |
| Deliverables | Product Solutions Product Expertise | Knowledge Strategies Outcomes |
| Communication | Performance Technical Detail Benefits Complex Industry Focused | Needs Strategies Value Outcomes Simplify the Complex Consumer-Focused Intimate |
| Process | Transactional A Sales Call | Consultative A Partnership |
| Role | A Salesperson | A True Advisor |

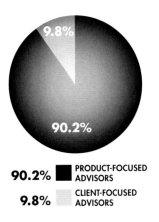

90.2% ■ PRODUCT-FOCUSED ADVISORS

9.8% CLIENT-FOCUSED ADVISORS

*Source: 2005 CEG Worldwide*

*"There is a growing disconnect between advisors and the changing needs of clients. More than 85% of advisors surveyed said they were "well prepared" to meet their clients [needs], while a majority of consumers surveyed disagreed."*

*2006 McKinsey & Company Report*

Noted strategist C.K. Prahalad talks about this disconnect between company thinking and consumer thinking in his recent book *The Future of Competition: Co-Creating Value at the Consumer Level* and argues that, because of the changing role of the consumer, companies that are best at co-creating value with consumers, unique to the context and needs of each, are the most successful - the very premise of a great advisory practice and this book.

The value-gap is further revealed in the earnings disparity between client-focused advisors and their product-focused brethren. There is a stark difference as 50% of client-focused advisors earned more than $500,000 in 2004 and none earned under $100,000. Conversely 45% of product-focused advisors earned less then $100,000 in 2004 while none earned over $500,000.
CEG Worldwide 2005

*The role of the consumer is changing*

*From isolated to connected*

*From unaware to informed*

*From passive to active*

*Resulting in a more connected, informed and active consumer.*

## Advisor Commentary

We've all seen these disconnects, either in our own practices or in that of others. And we know that those who best align their offerings and practice with needs of the client are probably the ones that are sitting in a corner office. I see these disconnects on a regular basis and even every so often in my own actions. Yet because we strive to run a truly client-focused business and focus on delivering the services and approach that today's consumer is looking for, we've been really successful, building a loyal and productive client base.

We are the only financial advisor to the majority of our clients and our inter-generational retention rates are 98%. And not only are we keeping our clients but we also see a steady flow of new clients and assets that we haven't necessarily pursued but instead they come to us. In 2008, arguable the toughest market in the last 70 years, we have brought on over $30 million in new assets.

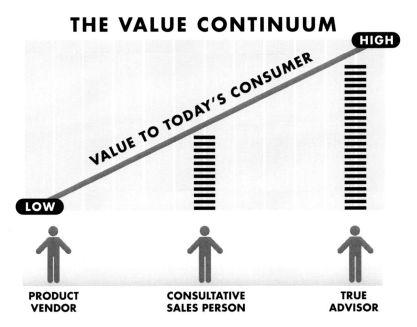

# THE VALUE CONTINUUM

**VALUE TO TODAY'S CONSUMER**

**HIGH**

**LOW**

| PRODUCT VENDOR | CONSULTATIVE SALES PERSON | TRUE ADVISOR |

While there are advisors who represent each end of this "value continuum" most advisor fall somewhere between. A root cause of this value gap is the entrenched "product-centricity" in the financial services industry – the reliance on product as the primary focus, source of competitive advantage and deliverable.

Product-focused practices are embedded in the industry's distribution structure, in advisor training, management direction, metrics and wholesaler support. With all that inertia and reinforcement it is not surprising that so many advisors employ product-focused business models and sales practices.

## Advisor Commentary

Production and net new asset requirements. Management direction. Wholesalers pitching product. It's not surprising that our industry has such a product-focused bent. Unfortunately the system is set up to fail the FA in too many ways to mention.

*"The key to future organic growth is product, product, product"*
*Senior Distribution Executive, Earnings Call, December 2006*

## THE CONSEQUENCES OF THE VALUE GAP

Consumer dissatisfaction or even worse consumer ambivalence are by-products of this value gap. Two recent studies support this. A 2008 Cogent Research study found that consumers more often than not use more than one advisor and a 2008 study by the Phoenix Companies found that 41% of affluent consumers surveyed don't use a financial advisor at all, the highest percentage in the seven-year history of the survey. Based on these findings, and the everyday experience of many advisors, it's clear that clients are harder to come by and less likely to be loyal. It doesn't take much to connect the dots and surmise that instead of attracting more affluent clients product-focused practices are driving them away.

Yet this value gap – these disconnects – aren't the only thing threatening the success of your practice. There's another significant market dynamic keeping advisors from fully participating in the affluent market – the inability to truly differentiate in a crowded and highly commoditized market. Both competitive convergence and strategic decay are at the root of this phenomenon.

## COMPETITIVE CONVERGENCE and STRATEGIC DECAY

Competitive convergence is a process that leads to commoditization and happens, ironically enough, in the quest to become better than the competition. Improvements to get ahead of the competition are quickly duplicated by the competition so instead of setting companies apart the quest to get better produces a continuous cycle of industry wide incremental improvements; repeating ever-converging operational improvements by everyone that ultimately creates no real sustainable advantages for anyone. To the consumer, everyone and everything begins to look the same and largely because everything is the same.

An advisors ability to differentiate and ultimately succeed with a product-focused business model is further hindered by strategic decay, the progressive loss in strategic capacity to create sustainable competitive advantages. Strategy is defined simply as a plan of action to achieve certain desired outcomes. Strategies are the way we get things done and, by nature, we can become very attached to our ways; that is the methods we use to achieve our goals. Yet strategies are not necessarily timeless and, in fact, often do lose their effectiveness.

Strategy guru Gary Hamel noted in the Harvard Business Review article *The Quest for Resilience* that historically "great companies", companies like Disney, Motorola, Sony and Hewlett-Packard "have apparently gone from great to merely okay". He found that because of increasingly turbulent times companies could no longer depend on "the flywheel of momentum to sustain their success" and ultimately that strategies that have driven success in the past are proving to be far less effective in the present.

Hamel suggests that a diligent, honest, and frequent review of the following questions will help one determine the effectiveness of a particular strategy, to test its resilience in the face of time and dynamic market conditions.

So ask yourself:

1) **Is my strategy losing its distinctiveness?**

2) **Is my strategy in danger of being superseded?**

3) **Is my strategy reaching the point of exhaustion?**

4) **Is increasing customer power reducing my margins?**

Let's answer these questions relative to product-focused strategies.

### 1) Is the strategy losing its distinctiveness?

Yes. With as many as 9 out of 10 financial advisors employing product-focused practices – in a highly commoditized product environment – their strategies have lost their ability to differentiate an advisor. This means that to consumers, more often than not, there is no discernible difference between one financial advisor and the next.

### 2) Is the strategy in danger of being superseded?

Yes. Consumers are looking for and choosing to work with someone other than product-focused advisors, advisors that offer more comprehensive and consultative services, services more akin to a professional service provider than a product salesperson.

### 3) Is the strategy reaching the point of exhaustion?

Yes. Product-focused strategies are no longer viable drivers of growth as consumers see little value in a salesperson with a product pitch.

### 4) Is increasing customer power reducing our margins?

Yes. Fee compression on commissioned and asset-based products along with legislative pressures reducing revenue streams are examples of this.

## A BLEAK FUTURE FOR PRODUCT-FOCUSED PRACTICES

The bottom line, as hard as it might be for some to hear, is product and specialty-focused business models and sales strategies are not satisfying the needs of today's marketplace. They are neither giving consumers what they want (or need) nor are they an adequate vehicle for advisors get to the next level in their practice, particularly if the goal is to attract more affluent consumers. Research supporting this reality revealed that a vast majority of advisors believe that a more comprehensive approach to providing financial advice will become the dominant business model. And from this, over 75% of the more successful advisors surmise there will be a thinning of the ranks, there will be fewer but much more successful advisors. So the progressive and ultimate shift to a financial services industry that provides more comprehensive, consultative and client-centric services is not a question of "if" but instead "when".

### Advisor Commentary

We take strategy very seriously not only at a client level but also at the business level. We recognize that our client-focused approach is what differentiates our business in the eyes of our clients. That and our actual ability to satisfy their needs are what attract the kind of clients we want.

At the same time we see far to many advisors that are product focused who are obviously lost in the crowd, trying to capture the attention of prospects with the latest great hot product or investment and having a hard time of it, particularly in tough markets. It seems pretty obvious that those advisors are in danger of drowning in obscurity and even moving on to their next career.

For those individuals (and companies) that want to thrive today, and in the future, employing more comprehensive, consultative and value-centric practices is not a choice but a necessity.

## FINALLY

So where are you on the value continuum? How well do your practices align with what your clients and prospective clients want and need? How effective is your strategy? Is the sustainability of your practice in danger? Is there an opportunity to capture more market share?

Knowing the answers to these questions is important and *The Seven Practices Toolkit*: Section One provides guidance to help give you a clearer understanding of where you are in your marketplace relative to your competition and the needs of the affluent consumer, the first step towards developing a more successful and sustainability advisory practice.

### Advisor Commentary

**Consumers are clearly taking a stand and taking control of their financial future. They are voting with their money and trust and only confiding in financial advisors that can provide them with what they're looking for, truly comprehensive and consultative services, advisors that can and are interested in making a real difference in their lives.**

# CHAPTER TWO

# The Seven Practices of High-Value Financial Service Professionals™

For many advisors attracting more affluent clients requires more than just incremental improvement. Instead it requires a fundamentally new business model – a business model focused on value and not product, one that provides a framework for offering the comprehensive services and consultative approach affluent

> *"Problems cannot be solved by thinking within the framework in which the problems were created"*
> – *Albert Einstein*

consumers are looking for. Being a true advisor, a true financial services professional, demands a business model more akin to a professional service provider than a salesperson.

Consumers recognize the value of engaging professional support to help in their quest to achieve their very intimate and important financial, life, retirement and legacy goals. They are looking for financial advisors that they believe will bring real value, advisors whom they feel they can trust. Consumers are looking for true strategic partners, true advisors who have the capacity to help them get the most from their wealth.

Are you a true advisor? Do your clients see you that way, your prospective clients? If not, as you learned in the first chapter, your future success is limited and the sustainability of your practice is most likely in danger. So what can you do to becomea true advisor? How can you further align your practice with the needs of the affluent, move further "up" the value continuum and attract more and better clients?

## THE SEVEN PRACTICES OF HIGH-VALUE FINANCIAL SERVICES PROFESSIONALS™

To help financial advisors bridge the value gap and realize greater success *The Seven Practices of High-Value Financial Services Professionals*™ provides a value-centric and client-focused business model that transcends product and imparts the key practices –

the perspectives, knowledge, language and processes – employed by the best in the industry.

*The Seven Practices* represent what top producers do to be true advisors, successfully attract affluent clients and build sustainable and thriving businesses. These fundamental practices are the building blocks for financial advisors and all those that support them to employ more client-focused, consultative, and compliant practices. They provide the path to helping you deliver the comprehensive services consumers need along with the consultative approach they want. Discerned through extensive observation, grounded in industry science and validated by top producers, *The Seven Practices* will help you:

## THE SEVEN PRACTICES
of High-Value Financial Services Professionals™

### THE PATH TO HIGHER PERFORMANCE

▲ Realign your business around value versus product

▲ Differentiate yourself in your marketplace

▲ Attract and retain more affluent clients

▲ Generate greater client satisfaction and loyalty

▲ Increase production and practice sustainability

▲ Better fulfill your fiduciary responsibilities

▲ Enjoy greater job satisfaction

# ORIGIN OF THE SEVEN PRACTICES

*The Seven Practices* are shaped from three primary sources;
1- Empirical Research;  2- Industry Science; and  3- Field Validation

## 1. The Seven Practices were discerned through empirical research

*The Seven Practices* were first discerned though extensive field observation and answers the fundamental question, "Why are the best the best?  What are the core competencies (knowledge, skills and attitudes) that make the most successful advisors, firms and wholesalers so successful?" *The Seven Practices* is a highly practical model firmly rooted in world of the financial services professional.

*Scientific Truth: A falsifiable hypotheses that has so far resisted falsification is a candidate for truth, the more extensive the failed efforts to falsify it, the better the candidate.*

## 2. The Seven Practices are grounded in industry science

Science, defined, is a branch of knowledge or study dealing with a body of facts or truths. It is scientific theory, the facts and truths that enables us to predict, often with high levels of certainty, the outcomes of actions and events. *The Seven Practices* are built upon and leverage time tested high performance theories from scientific disciplines that include organizational dynamics, competition theory, economics, innovation, branding, value chain optimization, organizational behavior, leadership and organizational learning. These proven and oft published (Harvard Business Review, MIT Sloan Journal) and oft used (in the Fortune 500 world) theories and associated processes provide the depth and rigor needed to help you make real and lasting change.

## 3. The Seven Practices have been validated by top producers

Finally *The Seven Practices* model has been and continues to be validated by those, the very best in the industry, which it represents.

Throughout my 20 plus years as a financial advisor I've seen the good, the bad and the ugly in terms of advisor practices and I've also been exposed to the very best. And this is it, The Seven Practices are a definitive description of what the best do, it's a career-changing business model for your practice. And really it's no secret because being client-focused is the way things should be done. It's what an advisory practice should be all about.

For us building a client-focused business has taken us to levels of success that we certainly envisioned but even beyond. It's the foundation and framework that keeps us connected with our clients and helps us exceed their expectations even in a market and world we can't control.

Being true advisors to our market – the culmination of employing The Seven Practices – has helped us attract great clients and build truly intimate relationships and we see this in how much our clients trust us, need us, and rely upon us. We notice the power of attraction even more in the tougher markets, as the more knowledgeable and informed consumers seem to only seek out advisors that have their best interests at heart, offer the comprehensive services they need and the highly consultative approach they want. Ultimately in good times or bad, the great clients are going to advisors that embody The Seven Practices.

*No firm has fully capitalized on [today's] opportunity [yet] a small number of emerging leaders are getting a head start by embracing a more client-centric view.*

*2006 McKinsey & Company Report*

## THE SEVEN PRACTICES OF HIGH-VALUE FINANCIAL SERVICES PROFESSIONALS™

*The Seven Practices* are not just 'techniques' for generating more production, but fundamental operating principles that when effectively employed lead to industry best performance. The following is a brief description of each, while Chapters Three through Nine will take an in-depth look at each.

### EMBRACE A CLIENT-FOCUSED STRATEGY

An individual's fundamental belief about what they do, what they have to offer, and the role they fill ultimately dictates what they actually do.

### PRACTICE 1

### BE DRIVEN TO HELP OTHERS SUCCEED

The most successful in the industry at both the retail and wholesale level operate with the genuine purpose to help their clients achieve greater success. Being driven or compelled to help others – to be other focused - is not a cliché, but a fundamental operating principle that provides both motivation and direction.

Wholly putting the best interests of clients before anything else is both a morally and strategically sound decision. It leverages the parable that those who put themselves last will be first, and the fact that exemplary customer service is a proven driver of market leadership and long-term business success.

### PRACTICE 2

### HAVE A DEEP UNDERSTANDING OF THE VALUE YOU OFFER

The most successful possess in-depth knowledge of the value inherent in their products and offerings in terms and language that resonate with consumers. They understand how that value can be used to help their clients optimize their wealth and realize their financial, life, retirement, and legacy goals.

### OFFER COMPREHENSIVE SERVICES

An understanding of the value one has to offer and the desire to help others succeed is important, yet it is the range of expertise and the tools and strategies in one's repertoire that determines the value that one can offer.

## PRACTICE 3

## HAVE IN-DEPTH KNOWLEDGE OF FINANCIAL PLANNING

Knowledge is power, and the best in the industry possesses in-depth knowledge of financial planning. They understand how comprehensive financial planning strategies (leveraging a diverse array of products) can be used to help consumers optimize their wealth and realize their life, retirement and legacy goals.

## PRACTICE 4

## DEVELOP HIGHLY EFFECTIVE STRATEGIES

The best are equipped with extremely effective strategies. Either on their own or through strategic partnerships true advisors offer the comprehensive services - strategies, processes, tools and support - that consumers need to fully realize their very important and intimate goals.

## MAXIMIZE YOUR MARKET IMPACT

One's ability to reach the marketplace and fully leverage market opportunities is critical to success.

## PRACTICE 5

## UTILIZE HIGH PERFORMANCE BUSINESS PROCESSES

The most successful in the industry utilize advanced strategic planning, branding, marketing, innovation and metrics to maximize their market impact and their practice success.

## BE A TRUE ADVISOR

How one approaches, communicates, and interacts with a client influences the value the clients sees in them and the extent to which they will allow one in to their lives.

## PRACTICE 6

## EFFECTIVELY CONVEY VALUE

The most successful in the industry simplify the complex process of financial planning and effectively communicate the value of their offerings in language and context that resonates deeply with affluent consumers.

## PRACTICE 7
## EMPLOY A CONSULTATIVE
## CLIENT-FOCUSED APPROACH

The best in the industry employ a client-focused consulting process that allows them to engage high-value prospects and uncover significant opportunities to bring real value through effective inquiry and meaningful dialogue. They craft powerful strategies that respond to the core needs of clients and communicate the value of the strategies and the underlying products in a way that resonates with the client's world, issues, and needs. And because of this more often than not, the best in the industry gain the client's agreement to implement the strategies thus resulting in greater success for all. The best in the industry are seen as trusted advisors by their clients – true strategic partners in their client's quest to realize their financial, life, retirement and legacy goals.

Regardless of where you are on the value continuum, *The Seven Practices* provides a framework to help you focus on and improve on the critical practices that are proven to drive high levels of success in the affuent marketplace.

So what can you do next?

## INTEGRATING THE SEVEN PRACTICES

Your path to integrating *The Seven Practices* into your business will depend on where you are on the value continuum. But regardless of whether you want to re-invent your practice or strengthen an already client-focused business model any change starts with the decision to do so. Yet even with the decision to move up the value continuum there is a significant barrier to integrating new practices and behaviors.

As we discussed in Chapter One product-focused business models and sales practices are deeply embedded in the financial services industry, they are the norm. As with any "cultural norm" there is tremendous inertia to keep the status quo, the pressure to do what you have always done and to do what everyone else is doing. This inertia can and often makes change difficult. So to help you break free from the gravitational pull of the industry's product-focused ways and expedite your transition to higher value and higher performance practices – here are five things you can do.

## HAVE ZEALOUS INTENT

The first step to lasting change is to have zealous intent; to believe in and be driven to change. Zealous is defined as "intense desire" and intent means moving towards a specific target or goal. Zealous intent is the intense desire to achieve a particular outcome. Zealous intent generates the enthusiasm and belief needed to uproot deeply embedded practices and behaviors. Zealous intent provides both the direction and motivation needed to adopt new ways of doing things.

*Culture: In the simplest terms a culture is defined by the perspectives, practices, metrics and behaviors deemed acceptable by the collective (role, organization, industry, society). What is deemed normal, what is measured, what is rewarded, and what is expected, all express what a culture is. Because what is normal is so deeply embedded and largely defines who we are, cultural change can be very difficult.*

## LET GO OF THE PAST

Once you're committed to change with passion and direction, the next step is to let go of the past. The inability to let go of the past, to realize that what has gotten you to where you are may not get you where you want to go is often the most challenging barrier to behavioral change, particularly for highly competitive and successful people. Letting go of the past takes reflection, "Is what I'm doing still optimal given today's market realities, are my practices still meeting the needs of those I serve and maximizing my success?" It requires humility, "I realize there may be a more effective productive way of doing things." And it requires genuine curiosity, "How might I go about changing what I do for the better, what haven't I thought about before?"

## REDEFINE YOUR METRICS

As expectations and desired results change, so must measurement and rewards. What you measure and reward truly validates what is important and what isn't. So measuring and rewarding higher performance practices and the outcomes associated to them – more affluent clients, more market share, more loyal clients, higher intergenerational retention rates, the mastery of more robust practices and behaviors, etc. – is vital. Production is still an important metric for a higher performing culture but sustainable increases in production is the ultimate metric.

## DEVELOP A SUPPORT SYSTEM

A good support system can help you accelerate your transition to higher value and higher performance practices. Your support system can include anyone with an interest in seeing you succeed and the insight to help you make it happen – partners, colleagues, wholesalers, and management. Those in your support system can help you; 1- Practice new skills; 2- Stay accountable; 3- Overcome barriers and; 4- Recognize and celebrate success.

## GIVE FULL AND SUSTAINED EFFORT

Building or strengthening your capacity to satisfy the wants and needs of affluent consumers requires a full time effort over the long term. *The Seven Practices* are not just techniques to be learned but fundamental operating principles to be embodied and lived. So while the application of each practice will, on their own, improve your performance it is the cumulative mastery of all *Seven Practices* that will transform you into the true advisor that consumers are actively looking for. And this can take time.

## THE DECISION

Gaining mastery of *The Seven Practices*, becoming the true advisor that attracts more affluent clients takes focus and dedication yet the reward for your efforts are great for you and the clients you serve. Ultimately, employing a more comprehensive and consultative business model starts with the decision to do so.

What are you going to do?

Building a high performance advisory practice takes real passion, a real desire to perform at the highest level.  Seeing our clients succeed is what drives our practice; it's what gets us up in the morning, to take care of people who want us, need us and that we care about. We made the decision to build a client-focused practice early on, and it is the reason why today we manage over $400 million in assets and even more importantly why we have been and continue to play a truly relevant and significant role in the live of our clients. I can't imagine why you wouldn't want to do the same thing.

So be diligent in your pursuit of a better practice, to being a true advisor.  Be open to new ways of thinking and doing things, be mindful as to what's important, what you measure.  Leverage your resources, particularly your wholesalers.  Get them to read the book, use them as coaches (the really good ones) and sponsors for training. Being a sought out financial advisor doesn't happen overnight. So put in the time and effort. Follow the steps in this book. Gravitate towards the best and work towards being better everyday – it'll be worth it.

# The Seven Practices Toolkit: Section One

The purpose of *The Seven Practices Toolkit* is to give you the tools and process needed to successful integrate *The Seven Practices* into your daily activities. You may choose to **use a journal to answer the questions offered, to document what you have learned and to capture your key insights.**

The first step you can take towards elevating your practice and attracting more affluent clients is to examine your current strategies and practices and answer two critical questions.

Does a value gap exist between your practice
and the needs of today's consumer?

Is your current strategy giving you
a competitive edge in the marketplace?

## 1) Where are you on the value continuum?

Use the following chart to evaluate your practice. Be objective in your analysis and if possible have others around you – managers, colleagues, and even clients – evaluate you as well. Note specific "artifacts" that point to either a product or client-focus – collateral material, interview process, practice values, etc.

**If you score from 7 – 14**
Your practice is in danger; change is not a choice. Up or out.

**If you score from 15 – 27**
You have a solid platform from which to elevate your success.

**If you score from 28 – 35**
You employ a business model aligned with what consumers want and need. You have an opportunity to further refine and elevate an already client-focused practice.

| VALUE GAP ANALYSIS | Product-Focused Business Model Attributes | Your Practice | Consumer Needs |
|---|---|---|---|
| Focus | Product Niche | 1 2 3 4 5 | Their Own Issues and Goals |
| Objective | Sell Product | 1 2 3 4 5 | Achieve Financial Goals and Realize Ideal Life |
| Expertise | Narrow and Deep Product Specific | 1 2 3 4 5 | Broad and Deep |
| Deliverables | Product Solutions Product Expertise | 1 2 3 4 5 | Knowledge Strategies Outcomes |
| Communication | Performance Technical Detail Benefits Complex Industry Focused | 1 2 3 4 5 | Needs Strategies Value Outcomes Simplify the Complex Consumer-Focused Intimate |
| Process | Transactional A Sales Call | 1 2 3 4 5 | Consultative A Partnership |
| Role | A Salesperson | 1 2 3 4 5 | A True Advisor |

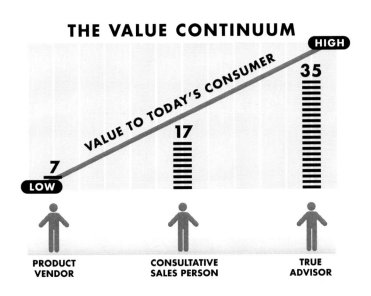

THE VALUE CONTINUUM

HIGH

VALUE TO TODAY'S CONSUMER

35

17

7

LOW

PRODUCT VENDOR

CONSULTATIVE SALES PERSON

TRUE ADVISOR

## 2) How effective is your current strategy?

Use the following questions to gauge the effectiveness of your current strategy.

Is your strategy losing its distinctiveness?

Does your strategy defy industry norms in any important ways?

Do you possess any competitive advantages that are unique?

Is your financial performance becoming less exceptional and more average?

Is your strategy in danger of being superseded?

Are there discontinuities (social, technical, or political) that could significantly reduce the economic power of your current business model?

Are there other business models that might render yours irrelevant?

Do you have strategies in place to co-opt or neutralize these forces of change?

Is your strategy reaching the point of exhaustion?

Is the pace of improvement in key performance metrics slowing down?

Are your markets getting saturated?

Are your customers becoming more fickle?

Is your company's growth rate decelerating, or about to start doing so?

Is increasing customer power eviscerating your margins?

To what extent do your margins depend on customer ignorance or inertia?

How quickly, and in what ways, are customers gaining additional bargaining power?

Do your productivity improvements fall to the bottom line, or are you forced to give them back to customers in the form of lower prices or better products and services at the same price?

Based on the analysis of your practice and strategy, is the sustainability of your practices in danger?

Is there an opportunity to further align your business model with market needs, to further differentiate your practice?

**If so the next step is to determine your readiness to change.**

## PREPARING FOR CHANGE

First determine the following for yourself, your team and your company.

1) **Do you have zealous intent?**

   Do you believe in the need to change?

   Do you understand why change is important?

   Do you want to change?

2) **Can you let go of the past?**

   Is what you're doing still optimal and is it maximizing your opportunity for success?

   Do you realize there may be a more effective and productive way of doing things?

   Are you interested in what you can do better, what you haven't thought about before?

## INFRASTRUCTURE DEVELOPMENT

Next broaden the metrics you use, beyond product knowledge, activity, and production to include:

▲ Affluence level of clients
▲ Percentage of client's assets
▲ Market share in target market
▲ Differentiation in market
▲ Brand strength
▲ Qualifying efficiency
▲ Client loyalty – retention plus referrals

- ▲ Inter-generational retention
- ▲ Progress towards mastery of more robust practices and behaviors

And finally begin to define your support system, how those around you can help you integrate and master *The Seven Practices*.

Partner(s):


Roles:


Managers:


Roles:


Colleagues:


Roles:


Wholesalers:


Roles:


Others:


Roles:

# My Plan For Change

# Embrace a Client-Focused Strategy

**PRACTICE 1**

Be Driven to Help
Others Succeed

**PRACTICE 2**

Have a Deep
Understanding
of the Value
You Offer

SECTION TWO provides insight
and guidance on employing Practices
1 & 2, the foundational practices of
the most successful financial advisors
in the industry.

CHAPTER THREE explores how
the best in the industry embrace a
client-focused strategy and have the
genuine desire to see their clients
succeed. It explores what today's
consumers both want and need to
succeed and what they really look
for in a financial advisor.

CHAPTER FOUR looks at the value
financial advisors can bring to their
clients. It provides comprehensive
value-centric language to help you
gain a deeper understanding of the
value you offer in terms that
resonate with consumers.

SECTION

# CHAPTER THREE

# Practice 1: Be Driven to Help Others Succeed

**Are you self-focused or other-focused?**

**Are you in it for your own good or for the good of others?**

> *"So the last shall be first, and the first last."*
>
> *–Matthew*

The path to becoming a true advisor and attracting more affluent clients starts with how you define your purpose and your role. As we saw in the last chapter the role of a product-focused advisor tends to be that of a salesperson, a salesperson whose purpose is to sell product with the goal of driving production and meeting personal quotas. In contrast the most successful financial advisors view their role as true advisors, real strategic partners with the sole purpose of providing the guidance, strategies, and solutions clients need to realize their very important and intimate financial and associated life goals. Top advisors operate with the genuine purpose to do the greatest good, with their client's best interest always ahead of their own. They are driven to help their clients succeed. This is the essence of Practice 1 and the fundamental point of divergence between the best and the rest.

**THE SEVEN PRACTICES**
of High-Value Financial Services Professionals™

THE PATH TO HIGHER PERFORMANCE

| 7 |
| 6 | Be A True Advisor | PRACTICE ⑥ ⑦ |
| 5 | Maximize Market Impact | PRACTICE ⑤ |
| 4 | Offer Comprehensive Services | |
| 3 | Embrace a Client-Focused Strategy | PRACTICE ③ ④ |
| 2 | | PRACTICE ❶ ❷ |
| 1 | |

PRACTICE 1 is both a directional beacon, a strategic compass for day-to-day decisions and a motivating force, as helping clients achieve their financial and life goals – important and intimate to each individual – is far more rewarding than "just" selling product. Practice 1 is not a cliché, but a fundamental operating principle best practiced with sincere desire and unwavering focus. It leverages the time tested truths that those who put themselves last will be first and that having an unparalleled focus on satisfying the customer is integral to long-term business success.

Becoming more client-focused starts with making the strategic decision to do so, the decision to drive your success by focusing on the success of the clients you serve. Again while this decision is certainly morally sound be clear that this is a strategic business decision, a plan of action designed to align your offerings with what affluent consumers want,

### Advisor Commentary

**Attracting more affluent clients means putting your goals and agenda aside and focusing on the what's important to them. If a client or prospect perceives that your not focused on their best interests they'll walk in a heartbeat. Affluent consumers are looking for advisors that care about them, I am truly talking about genuine care and consideration for their welfare, not feigned interest to sell something, that's where the money is flowing.**

to set you apart from the competition and ultimately to help you take your business to the next level. Practice 1 is the consummate win/win. You succeed when your clients succeed.

So what do consumers need to succeed?

### SATISFYING CONSUMER NEEDS

Your clients and prospective clients all want to achieve certain financial goals so they can in turn realize their life, retirement, and legacy goals. They all want to realize their own unique vision of the future, their picture of an ideal life. As a financial advisor you have the opportunity to help them achieve these very important and intimate goals, making your role extremely important as the relative success a client experiences has broad ramifications on their quality of life and of those around them.

So what do your clients need to do to best realize their financial, life, retirement and legacy goals?

## IS WEALTH MANAGEMENT THE ANSWER?

Wealth management, popular since the early 1990s, is an advanced type of financial planning that provides individuals and families with private banking, estate planning, asset management, legal service resources, trust management, investment management, taxation advice and portfolio management that is certainly a more comprehensive and client-focused service model. Wealth management was originally conceived as a service model for high net worth clients, a true niche model to serve the wealthiest few. While wealth management is a more comprehensive service model there are two fundamental flaws in the approach that prevent it from being the ideal solution across the affluence continuum.

First, the wealth management model operates on the underlying premise that, for the most part, sustainable wealth (live well off the interest and touch little or none of the principle) already exists. This may be true for some affluent consumers but certainly not most. Research from Case Western University actually shows that "lesser affluent" clients who are being serviced by traditional wealth management practices often feel like they're just "small players" and are accepting of what they believe is a lower level of service.

Another flaw in the wealth management model is that while focusing on investments, portfolio management and legacy planning, wealth management often excludes an area fundamental to the success of most affluent consumers – risk management and wealth protection. Noted industry consultant Jack Sharry of The Phoenix Companies agrees with this premise in arguing that incorporating risk management is not only important for the client's success but also to help advisors "avoid commoditization" and that by doing so advisors "will become *trusted advisors* rather than a commodity".

Ultimately wealth management, a business model designed to serve the wealthiest few, fails to satisfy the needs of many affuent consumers in both substance and approach.

# WEALTH OPTIMIZATION

An alternative to wealth management is weath optimization – a comprehensive service model that addresses the holistic needs of today's affluent consumer. Weath optimization is a service model designed to help people get the most out their money so they can best realize their ideal life and legacy. The path to helping consumers optimize their wealth is unique yet all share three fundamental needs.

**Protect their wealth from knowable
and unforeseen events**

**Maximize the growth potential
of their investible assets**

**Effectively draw upon and
distribute their wealth**

While each of the three components – protection, accumulation, and distribution – are important in their own right; it is the power of the three strategically intertwined that provides consumers with what they need to effectively achieve their financial goals and ultimately realize their ideal life.

Wealth optimization is what consumers need from the advisors they work with. But what do consumers want from the advisors they work with?

## Advisor Commentary

Since the beginning, I've embraced a wealth optimization model and did so because it's what I have always felt consumers, my clients, needed and because it was my point of differentiation in the marketplace Ultimately my purpose is to help clients realize the best life they can, to truly live out their hopes and dreams and to do so by helping clients protect, grow and use their money as efficiently and effectively as possible. This means offering the holistic services and advice they need to make it happen.

Often advisors are short-term focused and looking for the next opportunity to sell, yet our job it to look at the big picture, to look at the long view. But to many advisors get caught in the one-dimensional trap - selling what they know and monthly quotas while clients are trying to prepare for the future and thinking about their legacy. Clients and prospects with numerous FA relationships (and the more wealth they have, usually the more advisors have as well) are looking for one to emerge that can serve their holistic and comprehensive needs, to help them realize their goals, someone to work with the attorney and the CPA, to emerge as the quarterback. And the first one to do this wins all the assets.

This played out recently with a long-term client of ours, a physician nearing retirement. He maintained advisory relationships with our practice and another advisor, a "great friend" who was good at picking stock. We only worked with about 10% of the assets until he finally realized (we were finally able to covey) that we cared most about his retirement, his family and legacy and less about stretching for a 100-200 basis point excess return net of fees over the benchmark. Ultimately he came to the conclusion that while the other FA was a 'great friend' he never took the lead and we were a better choice for taking care of him and his family. We went from working with just 10% to all of the assets, over $7,000,000, because we understood that it wasn't about the hot performer but instead about the client's quality of life.

In the end there really was no competition, all the money flowed to the advisor (us) that could play a truly relevant and significant role in the client's life, an advisor that can help them optimize their wealth and realize their ideal life and legacy.

*Manage – to handle, direct, govern, or control. Origin: 1555–65; manege (Italian) - to handle and train horses*

*Optimize - to make as effective, perfect, or useful as possible. Origin: 1835 -45 from optimus (Latin) – best, ideal, or perfect*

## WHAT CONSUMERS WANT

There is a common belief that the two key drivers of client satisfaction are product performance and affinity. And while performance is of course on the consumers' radar screen, research from Case Western University reveals that the dynamic created by product-focused advisors pitching the latest "hot dot" while trying create a connection by "making a friend' with the prospect is more often than not going to repel the affluent consumer.

**Instead the things that are important to today's consumer, the things that drive consumer satisfaction are:**

1. The level of control they feel over the financial planning process and in the relationship with the advisor

2. Their perception of the value the advisor places on the relationship

3. The level of trust the consumer has for the advisor

4. Performance

**So from this we can determine what consumers really want are financial advisors:**

1. That simplifies the complex process of financial planning, advisors that truly help them grasp the concepts, ideas and strategies needed to  optimize their wealth;

2. That sincerely values the relationship, advisors that make them feel important, regardless of the size of their assets;

3. With integrity, advisors that they can trust to put their needs above everything else;

4. Who perform; advisors that consistently generate the outcomes are looking for.

Today's consumer, particularly the affluent, are looking for advisors that deliver on these fronts, that's where the money and client loyalty are flowing.

## THE DECISION

Being driven to help your clients succeed is the first step to being a true advisor and attracting more affluent clients. For many this requires a sincere change in heart, from being self-focused to being other-focused and from being product-focused to being client-focused. Successfully employing a client first strategy starts with fully understanding what consumers want and need from you and then charting a course to building your capacity to meet those wants and needs. It means committing to fulfilling the role of true advisor and doing what's necessary to get there.

Practice 1 is the first step on the path to greater success and sustainability. It is the fundamental point of divergence between client-focused and product-focused advisors. It is the fork in the road.

Which way are you going to go?

# CHAPTER FOUR

# Practice 2: Have a Deep Understanding of the Value You Offer

> *Knowledge is a process of piling up facts; wisdom lies in their simplification.*
>
> –*Martin H. Fischer*

Now that you understand what it means to embrace a client-focused strategy – with the greatest good and the best interests of your clients at heart – the next step to being a true advisor and achieving greater success is to understand the value you can offer to consumers in terms they understand, the specific things you can do to help clients optimize their wealth in language and context that resonates with them. This is Practice 2, the deep and thorough understanding of what financial advisors can do for clients relative to their needs and their world and the next point of divergence between the most successful and the rest.

## PRODUCT VERSUS CLIENT-FOCUSED ADVISOR ATTRIBUTES

Product-focused advisors generally view product, the associated features and benefits, and product expertise as the prime source of their value. Their goal is to sell and they define success primarily as the placement of a product in a client's portfolio. Conversely the most successful advisors understand that the real value they offer is the value inherent in the strategic use of financial products and services. Their goal is to fulfill and they define success as the accomplishments clients make towards realizing their goals. The goal of the best in the industry is leverage the value inherent in whatever financial products and services will help their clients overcome the barriers to achieving their financial goals and realizing their ideal life.

THE CONSUMERS
POINT OF VIEW

A fundamental concept of *The Seven Practices*, as a client-focused business model, is to see the world through the consumer's eyes, to understand how they think, to focus on the issues that matter to them and to ultimately provide meaningful and fruitful advice within the context of their world.

Because of this, interpreting what you do and defining your value in a way that makes sense to consumers is critical. As we saw in Chapter Three, clients want first and foremost to understand what can be the complex and overwhelming subject of financial planning. Helping clients satisfy this need takes more than just a spin on "industry and product-speak", it requires fluency in a comprehensive client and value-centric language.

THE CONSUMER EXPERIENCE
IN A PRODUCT-FOCUSED WORLD

The want guidance, maybe they are lost or just uncertain. Yet they are looking for help. Unfortunately they are in a foreign land, the native tongue unknown to them. They have sought help, yet as far as they can tell no one speaks their language nor understands what they need. Frustrated they give up and set out to find their way on their own.

# VALUE-CENTRIC LANGUAGE

The following "value-centric language" articulates how you can help clients optimize their wealth in language that makes sense to them. It provides a comprehensive definition of what financial products, services, and ultimately financial advisors do for consumers. Value-centric language is highly compliant language (not legal representative advice, check with your own compliance department) created and vetted in a collaborative effort with the field and field leadership. This client-focused language is made up of individual value statements that are powerful in their own right and are, in fact, the basis for a top advisors practice, their key deliverables. Yet when combined, the value statements create a robust client-focused language that describes everything you can do (and that financial services products do) in a way that resonates with consumers.

So how can you help your clients optimize their wealth? What can you do to help your clients get the most life from their wealth?

## Advisor Commentary

Language is everything and this is something a lot of advisors don't understand. Many don't take a look at the information that they're delivering from the clients point-of-view. Putting a strategy or solution together for your clients is just the beginning of the job. Your real task is to communicate the value of the proposed solution and get the client on board, to get them to act with confidence and do what they need to succeed.

Language is the most powerful tool we have to make that happen and communicating with clients in "consumer-speak" versus "industry-speak" is what helps us build strong, productive and loyal relationships. In fact my favorite kind of client is the one that doesn't think the proposed solution is "right" or maybe they've heard negative things about a particular product yet by effectively conveying the value of the solution in language that resonates with their core needs they understand why the solution is appropriate and buy in wholeheartedly.

Ultimately the value and client-focused language we use (along with our common goals) is what connects us to our clients.

## You Can Help Your Clients Protect their Wealth from Knowable and Unforeseen Events

The health and prosperity of ones financial future is far from guaranteed. There are events and risks that can slowly erode or even decimate a client's ability to realize their life goals. To combat these events and offset the risks that threaten the optimization of a client's wealth you can help your clients:

**Make appropriate investment decisions** and help them optimize their wealth by protecting them from the dangers inherent in over-weighted or misallocated portfolios due to an inadequate knowledge of what an appropriate investment decision is relative to their needs and from the emotional investment decisions that can come from fear or greed that is so much part of the human behavior in the investing process.

**Gain the confidence to take action and stay invested** and help them optimize their wealth by mitigating some of the risks inherent in investing and in life and protect them from making less than optimal investment decisions. This allows clients to be comfortable and at peace with taking and sticking with the appropriate actions needed to optimize their wealth.

**Have the comfort to know that they will never outlive their income** and help them optimize their wealth by protecting them from the fear of outliving their assets, and the associated stress and strain, and the reality of running out of money, and all of the significant and potentially dire ramifications that come along with that.

*Hermeneutics – The Science of Interpretation*

*There are very real differences in how people define meaning, how they interpret what they hear, see and read and these differences are greatly influenced by the context of the situation in which meaning is being conveyed and the receiver's worldview. Hermeneutics is the science of understanding things from somebody else's point of view, and to recognize the cultural and social forces that may have influenced their outlook.*

**Protect themselves from catastrophic events** and help them optimize their wealth by protecting them from the life or world events that can disrupt even the best-developed plan. Whether it's an unexpected death, a debilitating disability or illness or even a dramatic market downturn this protects clients from the events that can decimate the assets needed to at best still realize all their goals and at worst maintain choice, dignity and independence in times of great trial.

**Ensure the family's ability to maintain their lifestyle** and help them realize the financial and life goals by protecting them from the life and socioeconomic displacement that can result from a drastic change in ones financial health or life situation due to life and world events.

**Preserve freedom of choice** and help them protect themselves and their families from the significant reduction in quality-of-life caused the by financial inability to fund alternative choices regarding life and health issues. This helps clients maintain their dignity and independence throughout their lives regardless of circumstance.

**Retain the flexibility to continue transfer or sell business interests** and help them optimize their wealth by protecting them from the negative consequences of a forced-upon and potentially unwanted business partnership in the event of the death of a business owner and helps to facilitate a smooth business transition.

**Help them fulfill their desired legacy** and help them optimize their wealth by protecting them against the behavior, life, and world events that can threaten their wealth and inhibit their ability to leave the memory they want.

### You Can Help Facilitate the Growth Potential of Your Clients Investible Assets

Growing wealth is of course very important for most clients. Even the wealthiest want their money to grow even if it's to pass onto family, foundations and charities. So the next component to helping clients optimize their wealth is to get the most out of their investment opportunities and you can do so by helping clients:

**Control the timing and impact of their tax burden** and help clients optimize their wealth by minimizing current and future taxes, resulting in more money being compounded sooner, growing wealth, and fewer taxes paid later, providing more income.

**Have well-chosen investment selections regardless of risk** and help clients optimize their wealth by leveraging the knowledge, expertise and experience of proven and continuously screened money managers to generate consistent returns relative to risk. This gives clients both peace of mind and the strategic focus needed to realize their goals.

**Maximize investment diversification and efficiency** and help clients optimize their wealth by reducing the effect of volatility on the consistency of return relative to risk and by minimizing the tax consequences of intra-investment taxable events. This gives clients the opportunity to gain more consistent long-term results and accumulate more assets.

**Adapt their portfolios in response to changing market conditions and life events** and help clients optimize their wealth by ensuring a continual alignment between their life or the world context/reality and their investment strategy. This gives clients the ability to maximize their investment strategy regardless of life or world events.

**Leverage alternative strategies for retirement income** and help clients optimize their wealth by minimizing taxes and maximizing income through all available tax-advantaged long-term investment strategies.

## You Can Help Your Clients Effectively Draw Upon and Utilize their Wealth

This is the end game, the reason for the first two areas of focus, the ability to draw on wealth to realize one's ideal life and to do so with confidence and certainty. You can help clients:

**Have the choice of multiple income options and flexible income streams** and help clients realize their ideal life by providing income in a way that best suites their particular goals and life situation when they need or choose to draw on their wealth.

**Create predictable lifetime income** and help clients realize their ideal life by removing uncertainty in future income allowing them to focus on living the life they want with peace-of-mind.

**Enjoy their wealth without jeopardizing their legacy** and help clients realize their ideal life and desired legacy by letting them spend their wealth in their lifetime, enjoying the fruits of it, and still pass on wealth to future generations or important causes.

**Enhance wealth through a leveraging effect** and help clients realize their desired legacy by multiplying assets designated for inter-generational transfer or charitable giving allowing them to magnify the impact of their legacy.

**Transfer wealth in a tax efficient manner** and help clients realize their desired legacy by minimizing the effect of taxes on inter-generational transfer and maximizing their legacy.

**Create liquid capital needed to offset potential tax burdens** and help clients realize their desired legacy by protecting against a reduction in liquid assets or even the liquidation of "family heirloom" assets.

**Transfer their values, integrity, and work ethic to future generations** and help clients realize their desired legacy by doing the greatest good, passing on the values that made the wealth to the next generation so they will do the same for their next generation and continuing, ideally, in perpetuity.

## MAKING SENSE

*Relationships are built on connections, connections are created through dialogue and dialogue happens through common language.*

Value-centric language answers the question "what do you do?" with depth and clarity. It provides a tactical compass for you in your efforts to help clients and a meaningful and compelling description of what you do for clients. Value-centric language helps to satisfy the consumer's number one desire – to understand the complex process of financial planning and feel in control of the process. Arguably this capacity to articulate value from the consumer's point-of-view is the very basis for attracting and keeping more affluent clients.

## Advisor Commentary

Ultimately the way you communicate – the language you use – can make the difference between success and failure for you and your clients. If you don't effectively lay down the foundation and do the heavy lifting up front to ensure your clients clearly understand the what, why, and how of their financial plan and to make sure they have a firm grasp of the process you use, then when tough times hit – and they always do – emotion takes over. The exact opposite of what you and your clients need to succeed.

## SEEKING FLUENCY

So what can you do next? First recognize that these value statements are the basis for a great advisory practice, that they're the key deliverables that enable top advisors to satisfy the comprehensive needs of affluent consumers. Acknowledge that while effective on their own, the real power of these value statements is in their use as a client-focused language – comprehensive verbiage that conveys the value of what you do in a language and context that resonates with the clients you're looking for.

Next, commit to memorizing the verbiage and internalize its meaning, and as you do begin to integrate the language into your interactions with your clients and prospective clients, in both how you think about a client's issues (more on that in Chapter Nine) and in how you actually communicate (more on that in Chapter Eight). The ultimate goal is for you to understand the value you bring to your clients and for you to be able to effectively convey the value in a way that truly resonates with your clients world.

## FINALLY

Embracing a client-focused strategy is the basis for top advisor success and amongst other positive attributes is at the heart of building trust with clients. It does so by putting the clients' best interests first and by demystifying the complex process of financial planning, both attributes that affluent consumers are looking for in a financial advisor. Practices 1 and 2 are the very foundation on which you can build a more successful and sustainable business; they're the first steps towards the top.

## Advisor Commentary

Putting the best interests of our clients first, knowing who they are what they really need, really caring about them and knowing how to care for them is the foundation for the success of our practice. It differentiates us from the masses and draws the more affluent client to us. We really enjoy seeing our clients succeed and seeing them achieve their own unique financial, life and legacy goals. By doing so we get to realize our own financial and life goals. It's awesome; I can't imagine doing it any other way.

# The Seven Practices Toolkit: Section Two

## EMBRACING A CLIENT-FOCUSED STRATEGY

Mastery of Practice 1 and Practice 2 is the foundation of being a top advisor; being directed and motivated by an unwavering focus on your clients' best interests, along with a deep understanding of what you can do for them in terms they understand.

### Practice 1 – Be Driven to Help Others Succeed

Wealth Optimization is the combination of helping clients

1. _____

_____

2. _____

_____

3. _____

_____

What is the key difference between wealth management and wealth optimization?

Clients want to work with financial advisors that

1. _____

_____

2. _____

_____

3. _____

_____

4. _____

_____

**Practice 2 – Understanding Your Value**

What is the value of your current offerings?

Product/Service:

Value Attributes (from value-centric language)

Product/Service:

Value Attributes

Product/Service:

Value Attributes

# My Plan For Embracing A Client-Focused Strategy

# Offer Comprehensive Services

**PRACTICE 3**

Have In-Depth Knowledge of Financial Planning

**PRACTICE 4**

Equip Yourself with Highly Effective Strategies

Section Three explores Practices 3 and 4 and how the best begin to fulfill a client-focused strategy by offering the comprehensive services desired by today's consumers.

CHAPTER FIVE presents a comprehensive overview of the products used in financial planning and the value associated with each. This primer looks at the key features, fees, expenses and the specific value associated with each product, to help you effectively link product and the value inherent within it.

CHAPTER SIX provides the tools for creating effective strategies unique to the needs of each client. This chapter walks through the strategy development process with two relevant client scenarios.

SECTION

# CHAPTER FIVE

# Practice 3: Have In-Depth Knowledge of Financial Planning

Once you've made the strategic decision to put your clients first and you understand the value you can offer to help them optimize their wealth, the next step to being a true advisor is to build the capacity you need to deliver on that value; to develop the ability to offer the comprehensive services that affluent consumers are looking for and need. Building this capacity starts with a thorough understanding of the "tools"– the financial products and services available to you – and their inherent value in helping clients achieve their financial goals and ultimately realize their ideal lives. This in-depth knowledge is Practice 3 and the next point of divergence between top advisors and the rest.

> *"The good life is inspired by love and guided by knowledge"*
> –Bertrand Russell

## PRODUCT VERSUS CLIENT-FOCUSED ADVISOR ATTRIBUTES

Product-focused advisors, while being experts in their own product(s), are often limited in expertise and have little comfort with products outside their own specialty. Top advisors, in contrast, possess a broad and deep understanding of financial planning. They have comfort and expertise – or are partnered with someone who does – with all available products and services. They leverage whatever product or combinations of products that are suitable for helping each of their clients realize their unique goals.

All professions have "tools of the trade", yet as we know, it's not the tools themselves that are of value, but instead what those tools can do when used by someone with skill and expertise. This certainly holds true for financial advisors as your skill in using the value inherent in all financial products and services determines the extent to which you can help clients achieve their financial and life goals, and correspondingly your ability to attract the clients you want.

> *Something is expensive only in the absence of value; people are willing to pay for things they deem valuable*

## PRODUCTS AND THEIR VALUE

So to help you deepen your knowledge, to help you tie product and value together, the following is an overview of the key financial planning products available and the value inherent in each. The purpose of this fairly lengthy section is not to teach you what products are available, that's something you probably already know, nor is the purpose to teach the inner workings of every product, that would require a book all to its own. Instead the purpose of this section is to help you link features to value and value to cost. This will help you better understand and communicate the value of the products available and better communicate what clients get in return for the fees and expenses they pay.

Each product review 1– identifies the value propositions (from Practice 2) that the product helps to fulfill; 2– describes its key features along with costs and expenses; and lastly 3– links specific product features with their value in helping clients optimize their wealth and realize their ideal future.

One of the benefits of working with a good wholesaler is their in-depth product expertise, so leverage them to learn more about the inner workings and choices among product classes.

We'll take a look at annuities (SEG Funds), professionally managed money, life insurance, qualified plans (RSSPs), long-term care insurance, disability insurance and alternative investments.

# ANNUITIES

We're living longer and have the opportunity to enjoy more, yet we're doing so in times of greater volatility and uncertainty. In these dynamic times variable annuities offer significant value to consumers in their quest to realize their goals and dreams.

**Annuities can protect wealth from knowable and unforeseen events by helping clients:**

▲ Make appropriate investment decisions

▲ Gain the confidence to take action and stay invested

▲ Protect against catastrophic events

▲ Ensure the family's ability to maintain their lifestyle

**Annuities can facilitate the growth potential of investible assets by helping clients:**

▲ Control the timing and impact of their tax burden

▲ Provide well-chosen investment selections regardless of risk

▲ Maximize investment diversification and efficiency

▲ Adapt their portfolios in response to changing market conditions and life events

▲ Leverage alternative strategies for retirement income

**Annuities can effectively distribute wealth by helping clients:**

▲ Have the comfort to know that they will never outlive their income

▲ Have multiple income options and flexible payouts

▲ Have an opportunity to create predictable lifetime income

## WHAT IS AN ANNUITY?

A variable annuity is a contract between the owner and an insurance company, under which the insurer agrees to make periodic payments to owner, beginning either immediately or at some future date. A variable annuity has two phases: an **accumulation phase** and a **payout phase.**

During the accumulation phase, the owner makes purchase payments, which can be allocated to a number of investment options. However, if the owner withdraws money from their account during the early years of the accumulation phase, they may have to pay "surrender charges," which are discussed below. In addition, they may have to pay a 10% federal tax penalty if they withdraw money before the age of 59½.

At the beginning of the payout phase, owners may receive their purchase payments, plus investment income and gains (if any), as a lump-sum payment, or they may choose to receive them as a stream of payments at regular intervals (generally monthly). In addition, some annuity contracts are structured as immediate annuities, which means that there is no accumulation phase and owners will start receiving annuity payments right after they purchase the annuity.

## ANNUITY KEY FEATURES

### Death Benefit

If the owner dies before the insurer has started making payments, the beneficiary is guaranteed to receive a specified amount – typically at least the amount of the purchase payments.

### Step-up Death Benefit (optional)

The purpose of a stepped-up death benefit is to "lock in" your investment gains and prevent a later decline in the value of an account from eroding the amount left to heirs.

### Annuitization

This lets the owner receive periodic payments for a certain period of time, including the rest of their life or the life of their spouse or any other person that is designated.

### Tax-Deferred

That means owners pay no taxes on the income and investment gains from the annuity until they withdraw your money. They may also transfer money from one investment option to another within a variable annuity without paying tax at the time of the transfer.

## LIVING BENEFITS (ALL OPTIONAL)

### Guaranteed Minimum Income Benefits (GMIB)

A GMIB is exactly what the name implies—a guaranteed minimum level of annuity payments by the insurance company, regardless of the performance of your annuity. Guaranteed Minimum Income Benefits guarantee the greater of the actual value, 5-7% compounded annual interest (annuitized), or the highest contract anniversary value (annuitized).

### Lifetime Withdrawal Benefits (LWB)

A LWB allow you to take withdrawals from 4-8% per year for your entire lifetime, regardless of your account value.

### Guaranteed Minimum Withdrawal Benefits (GMWB)

Guaranteed Minimum Withdrawal Benefits permit you to withdraw up to 7% per year without the risk of losing your principal, regardless of market performance.

### Guaranteed Account Value Benefits (GAV)

Guaranteed Account Value Benefits guarantee the original investment, give you market upside, and allow you to take your investment as a lump sum after a certain period of time.

### Sub-Accounts

Very similar to mutual funds, yet with some different regulatory requirements, sub-accounts provide the same features as mutual funds, which include professional money management, diversification, asset allocation, and dollar cost averaging. See the key features for professionally managed money for more information.

Other features may include cost of living increase, premium return, nursing home, long-term care coverage, and disability wavers.

## ANNUITY FEES AND EXPENSES

### Surrender Charges

If the owner withdraws money from a variable annuity within a certain period after a purchase payment (typically within six to eight years, but sometimes as long as ten years), the insurance company usually will assess a "surrender" charge, which is a type of sales charge.

### Mortality and Expense Risk Charge

This charge is equal to a certain percentage of your account value, typically in the range of 1.25% per year. This charge compensates the insurance company for insurance risks it assumes under the annuity contract.

### Administrative Fees

The insurer may deduct charges to cover record-keeping and other administrative expenses. This may be charged as a flat account maintenance fee (perhaps $25 or $30 per year) or as a percentage of your account value (typically in the range of 0.15% per year).

### Underlying Fund Expenses

The fees and expenses imposed by the mutual funds that are the underlying investment options for the variable annuity.

### Fees and Charges for Other Features

Special features offered by some variable annuities, such as a stepped-up death benefit or a living benefit carry additional fees and charges. Other charges, such as initial sales loads, or fees for transferring part of your account from one investment option to another, may also apply.

## THE VALUE OF ANNUITIES

What can annuities do to help your clients optimize their wealth? What do your clients get for the fees and expenses they pay? In times of greater longevity, greater volatility and future uncertainty annuities can be highly effective tools in helping your clients optimize their wealth.

**Annuities can help your clients protect their wealth from knowable and unforeseen events by helping them:**

▲ **Make appropriate investment decisions** by providing effective investment guidance through **professional money management** and future certainty and guarantees through **living benefits**. This protects clients from the dangers inherent in over-weighted or miss-allocated portfolios and from the emotional investment decisions that can come from fear and greed that drives people in and out of the market, significantly reducing their long-term returns.

▲  **Gain the confidence to take action and stay invested** by providing effective investment guidance through **professional money management** and future certainty and guarantees through **living benefits.** This helps clients mitigate some of the risks inherent in investing and in life and protects them from making less then optimal investment decisions. It allows them to be at peace with taking and sticking with the appropriate actions needed to optimize their wealth.

▲  **Be protected from catastrophic events** by providing guaranteed retirement income through **living benefits.** This protects clients against severe market loss and at best still will still allow them to realize all their goals and, at worst, maintain choice, dignity, and independence in times of great trial.

▲  **Ensure their family's ability to maintain their lifestyle** by providing guarantees and certainty through **death benefits, living benefits, and annuitization.** This protects clients from the life and socioeconomic displacement that can result from a drastic change in ones financial health or life situation due to life and world events.

**Annuities can help your clients facilitate the growth potential of their investible assets by helping them:**

▲  **Control the timing and impact of their tax burden** by minimizing current and future taxes through **tax deferral.** This gives clients the opportunity for more money being compounded sooner; growing wealth, and fewer taxes paid later providing more income.

▲  **Have well-chosen investment selections regardless of risk** by leveraging proven knowledge, expertise and experience to generate consistent returns relative to risk through **professional money management.** This gives clients both peace of mind and the strategic focus needed to realize their goals.

▲  **Maximize investment diversification and efficiency** by reducing the effect of volatility on the consistency of return relative to risk and by minimizing the tax consequences of intra-investment taxable events through **tax deferral, asset allocation and dollar cost averaging.**

▲  **Adapt their portfolios in response to changing market conditions and life events** by ensuring a continual alignment between a client's life or the world context/reality and their investment strategy through **professional money management** across the risk spectrum.

▲  **Leverage alternative strategies for retirement income** by minimizing taxes and maximizing income through **tax deferral and** professional money management. This helps clients augment existing retirement assets and fill any gaps in desired income.

**Annuities can help your clients effectively draw upon and utilize their wealth by helping them:**

▲ **Maintain flexibility for drawing on retirement income** by providing multiple income options and flexible income streams through **annuitization and living benefits.** This helps clients draw on their income in a way that best suites their particular goals and life situation.

▲ **Have the comfort to know that they will never outlive their income** by providing guaranteed lifetime retirement income through **annuitization** and **living benefits.** This protects clients from the fear of outliving their assets, and the associated stress and strain, and the reality of running out of money and all of the significant and potentially dire ramifications that come along with that.

▲ **Have an opportunity to create predictable lifetime income** by providing a guaranteed income stream through **annuitization** and **living benefits.** This helps clients optimize their wealth by removing uncertainty in future income and allowing them to focus on living the life they want with peace-of-mind.

## PROFESSIONALLY MANAGED MONEY

Ever present and universally used, professional money management is a robust tool to help consumers optimize their wealth. Professional money management comes in numerous forms, from the ubiquitous mutual fund to separately managed accounts, and helps consumers optimize their wealth in the following ways.

**Professionally managed money can protect wealth from knowable an unforeseen events by helping clients:**

▲ Make appropriate investment decisions

▲ Gain the confidence to take action and stay invested

**Professionally managed money can help facilitate the growth potential of investible assets by helping clients:**

▲ Have well-chosen investment selections regardless of risk

▲ Maximize investment diversification and efficiency

▲ Adapt their portfolios in response to changing market conditions and life events

Managed money is just that – money managed by investment professionals either by pooling the assets of numerous clients as in mutual finds or managing them separately as in separately managed accounts (SMAs).

## KEY FEATURES OF PROFESSIONALLY MANAGED MONEY

### Professional Investment Management
By pooling the funds of thousands of investors, mutual funds provide full-time, high-level professional management that few individual investors can afford to obtain independently. Such management is vital to achieving results in today's complex markets. Fund managers' interests are tied to consumers because their compensation is based on how well the fund performs.

### Diversification
Mutual funds invest in a broad range of securities. This limits investment risk by reducing the effect of a possible decline in the value of any one security. Mutual fund shareowners can benefit from diversification techniques usually available only to investors wealthy enough to buy significant positions in a wide variety of securities.

### Tax Exempt
Certain mutual funds offer tax-exempt income at the local, state and federal level.

### Asset Allocation
Asset allocation is an investment portfolio technique that aims to balance risk and create diversification by dividing assets among major categories such as cash, bonds, stocks, real estate, and derivatives. Each asset class has different levels of return and risk, so each will behave differently over time.

### Dollar Cost Averaging
Dollar-cost averaging is a very simple method of investing that can often allow one to increase the overall value of their portfolio while reducing risk. Dollar-cost averaging works best in volatile markets, when prices are not in a continually rising pattern. To dollar-cost average, you invest a fixed amount of money on a regular schedule, usually every month. Since share prices fluctuate, you can end up buying more shares when the price is low, and fewer when it is high. Over time, you may accumulate more shares than if you had invested in one lump sum, at a lower average cost per share.

# PROFESSIONALLY MANAGED MONEY FEES AND EXPENSE

### A Shares
Typically called load fund, these funds are sold with an initial or front-end sales charge (usually 3-6%) that is deducted from the initial investment. Also, these funds most always charge a 12b-1 marketing fee (on average, around 0.25%), which is deducted from the fund's assets each year.

### B Shares
These funds have no front-end sales charge, but carry a redemption fee, or back-end load that is paid if the shares are redeemed within a certain number of years. This load (called a CDSC or contingent deferred sales charge) declines every year until it disappears-usually after six years. "B" share funds also carry a 12b-1 marketing fee which is typically higher than the 12b-1 fee of A shares.

### C Shares
Know as a "level-load" share, C shares have no front-end sales charge and no redemption fee, but they carry a 12b-1 marketing fee which you pay for as long as you hold the fund. It is similar to no-load funds that charge 12b-1 fees.

### Management Fees and Operating Expenses
All mutual funds, regardless of whether they are load or no-load, have management fees and operating expenses. It is the amount that the fund pays to the investment adviser for managing the fund's portfolio or providing other services, such as maintaining shareholder records or furnishing shareholder statements and reports. These fees are reflected in the fund's share price and are not charged directly to the shareholder. The management fee usually ranges from 0.5% to 1% of the fund's total asset value but may be higher for specialized funds.

### 12b-1 Fee
Named for the Securities and Exchange Commission (SEC) rule that originated it, a 12b-1 fee permits a fund to pay some or all of the costs of distributing its shares to the public. Some of these plans provide for payment of specific expenses such as advertising, sales literature, and sales incentives. They are not hidden charges and are explained in the fund's prospectus. For a fund to be called "no-load" its 12b-1 fee must not exceed 0.25% of assets.

**Redemption Fees**

Some funds charge a fee when shares are redeemed (sold) or exchanged for shares of another fund from the same company. This can be a simple fee at redemption or an exchange fee, or a contingent deferred sales charge (CDSC).

**Expense Ratio**

The expense ratio is the ratio of total expenses to net assets of the fund and includes management fees, 12b-1 charges if any, the cost of shareholder mailings and other administrative expenses. The ratio is often a function of the fund's size, rather than the operating efficiency of the fund management, but can also depend on the nature of the investments in the fund.

## THE VALUE OF PROFESSIONALLY MANAGED MONEY

What can professionally managed money do to help your clients optimize their wealth? What do your clients get for the fees and expenses they pay? Whether a SMA, embedded in a variable product or the ubiquitous mutual fund, managed money is the engine that drives growth for the vast majority of consumers and is a robust tool to help them realize their goals and dreams.

**Professionally managed money can help your clients protect their wealth from knowable and unforeseen events by helping them:**

▲  **Make appropriate investment decisions** by providing effective investment guidance through **professional money management and asset allocation.** This protects clients from the dangers inherent in over-weighted or miss allocated portfolios.

▲  **Gain the confidence to take action and stay invested** by providing effective investment guidance through **professional money management and diversification,** which allows clients to be at peace with the care and direction of their investment relative to risk.

**Professionally managed money can help facilitate the growth potential of your clients investible assets by helping them:**

▲  **Control the timing and impact of their tax burden** by eliminating some or all taxes paid on income through **tax-exempt funds.** This gives clients the opportunity to realize higher net returns relative to risk.

▲  **Have well-chosen investment selections regardless of risk** by leveraging proven knowledge, expertise and experience to generate consistent returns relative to risk through **professional money** management and diversification. This gives clients both peace of mind and the strategic focus needed to realize their goals.

▲ **Maximize investment diversification and efficiency** by reducing the effect of volatility on the consistency of return relative to risk and by minimizing the tax consequences of intra-investment taxable events through **professional money management, asset allocation and dollar cost averaging.** This gives clients the opportunity to gain more consistent results and accumulate more assets over the long term.

▲ **Adapt their portfolios in response to changing market conditions and life events** by ensuring a continual alignment between a client's life or the world context/reality and their investment strategy through **professional money management and asset allocation.** This helps clients maximize their investment strategy regardless of life or world events.

## LIFE INSURANCE

Life insurance, an often shunned and seemingly complex product, is an extremely robust tool for helping clients optimize their wealth.

**Life insurance can protect wealth from knowable and unforeseen events by helping clients:**

▲ Make appropriate investment decisions

▲ Gain the confidence to take action and stay invested

▲ Protect them from catastrophic events

▲ Ensure the family's ability to maintain their lifestyle

**Life insurance can clients facilitate the growth potential of investible by helping clients:**

▲ Control the timing and impact of their tax burden

▲ Have well-chosen investment selections regardless of risk

▲ Maximize investment diversification and efficiency

▲ Adapt their portfolios in response to changing market conditions and life events

**Life insurance can effectively distribute wealth by helping clients:**

▲ Leverage alternative strategies for retirement income

▲ Facilitate the desired distribution and utilization of their assets

▲ Enjoy their wealth without jeopardizing their legacy

▲ Enhance wealth through a leveraging effect

▲ Transfer wealth in a tax efficient manner

▲ Create liquid capital needed to offset potential tax burdens

▲ Transfer the value, integrity, and work ethic to future generations

**Life insurance** or **life assurance** is a contract between the policy owner and the insurer, where the insurer agrees to pay a sum of money upon the occurrence of the insured individual's or individuals' death or other event, such as terminal illness or critical illness. In return, the policy owner (or policy payer) agrees to pay a stipulated amount called a premium at regular intervals or in lump sums.

## LIFE INSURANCE KEY FEATURES

### Income-Tax-Free Death Benefit

The death benefit of a life insurance policy is passed on to beneficiaries free from federal income tax.

### Tax-Advantaged Growth

Any earnings accumulated in a insurance policy's cash value grow free from taxes until withdrawn. Please note that in a variable life insurance policy, cash value growth is not guaranteed.

### Tax-Advantaged Income

You may generally take income-tax-free distributions against the cash value of a life insurance policy, which is not a modified endowment contract (MEC). Special rules apply to modified endowment contracts and to certain withdrawals taken during the policy's first 15 years.

### Tax-Free Transfers

Transfers among the underlying investment options of a variable life or variable universal life insurance policy are not subject to current income or capital gains taxes.

### No Early Withdrawal Penalty

You can take loans or withdrawals from a life insurance policy prior to age 59½ without the 10% early withdrawal penalty (as long as the policy is not a MEC) that may apply to IRAs, 401(k)s, and other tax-deferred retirement plans or annuities.

### Sub Accounts (Variable Life Insurance)

Very similar to mutual funds yet with some different regulatory requirements, sub-accounts provide the same features as mutual funds, which include professional money management, diversification, asset allocation, and dollar cost averaging. See the key features of professionally managed money for more information.

## LIFE INSURANCE FEES AND EXPENSES

### Premium Loads/Sales Charges

These compensate the insurance company for sales expenses, state and local taxes. These charges are deducted from your premium payment before it is applied to the policy.

### Administration Fees

These are used to pay the costs of maintaining the policy, including accounting and record keeping. Administration fees usually are deducted from your policy value once a month.

### Mortality and Expense Risk Charges

When a policy is issued, the insurance company assumes the insured person will live to a certain age based on their current age, gender and health conditions. This charge compensates the insurance company in the case the insured person doesn't live to the assumed age. It is generally charged once a month.

### Cost of Insurance

This is the cost of actually having insurance protection. It is based on the insured person's age, gender, health and death benefit amount. Cost of insurance is also usually charged once a month.

### Surrender Charges

This charge is deducted from the cash value if the policy is surrendered (terminated) during the surrender charge period.

### Monthly per Thousand Charge

This charge is based on the insured person's age, gender, and underwriting classification and is assessed monthly.

### Fund Management Fees

These charges compensate the fund managers for their work. Fund management fees are usually deducted from the price paid for the shares of underlying fund options and not directly from your cash value.

# THE VALUE OF LIFE INSURANCE

What can life insurance do to help your clients optimize their wealth? What do your clients get for the fees and expenses they pay? Life insurance is a robust tool for helping your clients realize their goals and dreams.

**Life insurance can help your clients protect their wealth from knowable and unforeseen events by helping them:**

▲  **Make appropriate investment decisions** by providing effective investment guidance through **professional money management and asset allocation.** This protects clients from the dangers inherent in over-weighted or miss allocated portfolios due. (Variable Life Insurance)

▲  **Gain the confidence to take action and stay invested** by providing effective investment guidance through **professional money management** and **diversification**, which allows clients to be at peace with the care and direction of their investment relative to risk. (Variable Life Insurance)

▲  **Protect their families standard of living and future goals from catastrophic events** by providing the assets needed to replace lost future income through **death benefits.** This helps families at best still realize their financial and life goals and at worst maintain choice, dignity, and independence in times of great trial.

▲  **Ensures their family's ability to maintain their lifestyle** by protecting them from the life and socioeconomic displacement due to an "un-timely" death through **death benefits.**

▲  **Preserve freedom of choice** by protecting them from the significant reduction in quality of life caused by the loss of current and future income through **death benefits.** This helps clients maintain their dignity and independence throughout their lives regardless of circumstance.

▲  **Retain the flexibility to continue transfer or sell business interests** by protecting clients from the negative consequences of a forced upon and potentially unwanted business partnership in the event of the death of a business owner through **death benefits.** This helps clients facilitate a smooth business transition and minimizes the financial impact of a death.

▲ **Fulfill their desired legacy** by protecting them against the sudden loss of current and future income or by enhancing their wealth through **death benefits**. This helps clients leave the memory they want.

**Life insurance can help your clients facilitate the growth potential of their investible assets by helping them:**

▲ **Control the timing and impact of their tax burden** by minimizing current and future taxes through **tax advantaged growth and income**. This means more money being compounded sooner, growing wealth, and fewer taxes paid later providing more income.

▲ **Have well-chosen investment selections regardless of risk** by leveraging the knowledge, expertise, and experience of **professional money management** to generate consistent returns relative to risk. This gives clients both peace of mind and the strategic focus needed to realize their goals. (Variable Life Insurance)

▲ **Maximize investment diversification and efficiency** by reducing the effect of volatility on the consistency of return relative to risk and by minimizing the tax consequences of intra-investment taxable events through **professional money management, diversification, asset allocation, dollar cost averaging and tax advantaged growth**. This gives clients the opportunity to gain more consistent long-term results and accumulate more assets. (Variable Life Insurance)

▲ **Adapt their portfolios in response to changing market conditions and life events** by ensuring a continual alignment between their life or the world context/reality and their investment strategy through **professional money management and asset allocation**. This gives clients the ability to maximize their investment strategy regardless of life or world events. (Variable Life Insurance)

▲ **Leverage alternative strategies for retirement income** by minimizing taxes and maximizing income through **tax advantaged growth and income, professional money management, diversification, and dollar cost averaging**. This helps clients augment existing retirement assets as efficiently as possible.

**Life insurance can help your clients effectively distribute and utilize their wealth by helping them:**

▲ **Have multiple income options and flexible payouts** by accessing income in a way that best suites their particular goals and life situation when they need or choose to draw on their wealth through **tax advantaged income.**

▲ **Enjoy their wealth without jeopardizing their legacy** by letting them spend their wealth in their lifetime, and still pass on wealth to future generations or important causes through **death benefits.** This allows clients to enjoy the fruits of their labor while still passing on a meaningful legacy.

▲ **Enhance wealth through a leveraging effect** by multiplying assets designated for inter-generational transfer or charitable giving through **death benefits.** This helps clients magnify the impact of their legacy.

▲ **Transfer wealth in a tax efficient manner** by minimizing the effect of taxes on inter-generational transfer through **death benefits,** again helping clients maximize their legacy.

▲ **Create liquid capital needed to offset potential tax burdens** by protecting against a reduction in liquid assets or through **death benefits.** This allows clients to avoid the liquidation of "family heirloom" assets.

▲ **Transfer the value, integrity, and work ethic to future generations** and doing the greatest good, passing on the values that made the wealth to the next generation through **death benefits, life insurance trusts** and other estate planning techniques.

## QUALIFIED INVESTMENTS

"Qualified" investments – SEPs, 401(k) plans (defined contribution), defined benefit plans and IRAs – all enjoy tax favored status from the federal government and coupled with their underlying investments are effective tools in helping clients optimize their wealth.

**Qualified investments can protect wealth from knowable and unforeseen events by helping clients:**

▲ Make appropriate investment decisions

▲ Gain the confidence to take action and stay invested

▲ Protect them from catastrophic events

Qualified investments can help facilitate the growth potential of investable assets by helping clients:

▲ Control the timing and impact of their tax burden

▲ Provide well-chosen investment selections regardless of risk

▲ Maximize investment diversification and efficiency

▲ Adapt their portfolios in response to changing market conditions and life events

▲ Provide alternative strategies for retirement income

## KEY FEATURES OF QUALIFIED INVESTMENTS

### Pretax Contributions
Contributions to a qualified plan (both employer and employee) are made on a pretax basis (beginning in 2006, employers can allow employees to make after-tax "Roth" contributions to a 401(k) plan). You don't pay income tax on amounts contributed until you withdraw money from the plan.

### Tax-Deferred Growth
Investment earnings (e.g., dividends and interest) on all contributions grow tax deferred. Again, you don't pay income tax on those earnings until you withdraw money from the plan.

### Creditor Protection
In most cases, your creditors cannot reach your qualified retirement plan funds to satisfy your debts.

### Employer Matching
In some cases employers match a certain percentage of the employee's contribution.

## QUALIFIED PLAN FEES AND EXPENSES

Fees and expenses vary based on the vehicle; the following are expenses for 401(k) plans.

### Plan Administration Fees
The day-to-day operation of a 401(k) plan involves expenses for basic administrative services – such as plan record keeping, accounting, legal, and trustee services – that are necessary for administering the plan as a whole.

**Investment Fees**
By far the largest component of 401(k) plan fees and expenses are associated with managing plan investments. Fees for investment management and other investment-related services generally are assessed as a percentage of assets invested. See fees and expenses for professionally managed money for more information.

**Individual Service Fees**
In addition to overall administrative expenses, there may be individual service fees associated with optional features offered under a 401(k) plan. Individual service fees are charged separately to the accounts of individuals who choose to take advantage of a particular plan feature.

**Other Fees**
This category covers services, such as record keeping, furnishing statements, toll-free telephone numbers, and investment advice, involved in the day-to-day management of investment products. They may be stated either as a flat fee or as a percentage of the amount of assets invested in the fund.

## THE VALUE OF QUALIFIED PLANS

What can qualified investments do to help your clients optimize their wealth? What do your clients get for the fees and expenses they pay? Qualified plans are highly tax efficient investments that are very effective tools in helping clients optimize their wealth.

**Qualified investments can help your clients protect their wealth from knowable and unforeseen events by helping them:**

▲ **Make appropriate investment decisions** by providing effective investment guidance through **professional money management and asset allocation.** This protects clients from the dangers inherent in over-weighted or miss-allocated portfolios.

▲ **Gain the confidence to take action and stay invested** by providing effective investment guidance through **professional money management and diversification,** which allows clients to be at peace with the care and direction of their investment relative to risk.

▲ **Protect their wealth from catastrophic events** by protecting the assets from judgments and creditors through **creditor protection.** This helps clients at best still maintain choice, dignity, and independence in times of trial.

Qualified investments can help your clients facilitate the growth potential of their investible assets by helping them:

▲ **Control the timing and impact of their tax burden** by minimizing current and future taxes through **tax advantaged growth and income.** This means more money being compounded sooner, growing wealth, and fewer taxes paid later providing more income.

▲ **Have well-chosen investment selections regardless of risk** by leveraging the knowledge, expertise, and experience of **professional money management** to generate consistent returns relative to risk. This gives clients both peace-of-mind and the strategic focus needed to realize their goals.

▲ **Maximize investment diversification and efficiency** by reducing the effect of volatility on the consistency of return relative to risk, and by minimizing the tax consequences of intra-investment taxable events through **professional money management, diversification, asset allocation, dollar cost averaging,** and **tax advantaged growth.** This gives clients the opportunity to gain more consistent long-term results and accumulate more assets.

▲ **Adapt their portfolios in response to changing market conditions and life events** by ensuring a continual alignment between their life or the world context/reality and their investment strategy through **professional money management** and **asset allocation.** This gives clients the ability to maximize their investment strategy regardless of life or world events.

▲ **Leverage alternative strategies for retirement income** by minimizing taxes and maximizing income through **tax advantaged growth and income, professional money management, diversification, and dollar cost averaging.** This helps clients augment existing retirement assets as efficiently as possible.

## DISABILITY INSURANCE

A client's ability to generate wealth can be decimated by a catastrophic disability, disability insurance is a powerful tool to protect against such an event.

**Disability insurance can help protect wealth from knowable and unforeseen events by helping clients:**

▲ Protect themselves and family from catastrophic events

▲ Ensure the family's ability to maintain their lifestyle

- ▲ Protect themselves and family from catastrophic events
- ▲ Ensure the family's ability to maintain their lifestyle
- ▲ Preserve freedom of choice

Disability Insurance provides an income replacement benefit to the policyholder in the event they are unable to work because of an illness or accident.

## KEY FEATURES OF DISABILITY INSURANCE

**Own or Any Occupation**
A definition used to determine level of disability. With "own occupation," as the definition, you can begin to receive benefits from your policy if you are unable to perform the duties of your current job, with "any occupation" a person must be unable to engage in ANY meaningful work in order to start receiving benefits.

**Benefit Percentage**
Your disability benefit will be a percentage of your average pay, often over the past three years, usually from 50% to 80%.

**Benefit Period**
You can choose a policy that lasts only a few years, or you can choose "unlimited," meaning your disability income will last the rest of your life, or at least until you are eligible for social security.

**Elimination Period**
The elimination period is like a time deductible. It may be from 30 days to 6 months, depending on how much premium you want to pay. A longer elimination period will give you a lower premium. Benefit is not paid out until you have satisfied the elimination period. Some policies, however, will return the premium paid during the elimination period.

**Guaranteed Renewability**
The right to keep your policy no matter how many times you have to use it.

**Indexing**
Indexing could be thought of as inflation protection. Usually a person's income goes up over time. The indexing allows you to receive a benefit based on your years of income immediately preceding the onset of disability rather than on the income you may have had when you purchased the policy.

### Premium Waiver

Most companies waive your premium once you have been collecting your benefit for 60 to 90 days. Some will also return the premium you paid during the waiting period.

### Presumptive Disability

Refers to disabilities that occur suddenly, such as that which might result from a car accident. If the disability is irrecoverable and permanent, involving the loss of limbs, sight, hearing or speech, the presumptive clause in the policy will allow you to collect from the first day, thus avoiding the waiting period.

### Residual Disability Insurance

A provision that allows you to continue to collect at a reduced benefit once you get back to work. It assumes that you will not be able to resume all of your duties and get your income back up to what it was immediately. Thus you are able to collect some disability even when you begin to earn a wage.

### Return of Premium Rider

If you never use your policy, some companies will give your premium back over time.

### Survivor Benefit

This is a lump sum that is paid to a beneficiary upon the death of the insured. It is available as a rider and can be either a return of premium (for someone who never had to used the benefit) or a lump sum payout if a person dies while receiving benefits.

## DISABILITY INSURANCE FEES AND EXPENSES

### Premium

Disability insurance premiums are based on the client's age and health along with the policy design, any or own occupation, benefit amounts and periods, along with the length of the elimination period.

## THE VALUE OF DISABILITY INSURANCE

What can disability insurance do to help your clients optimize their wealth? What do your clients get for the premiums they pay? If current income is an important part of future wealth, disability insurance is a powerful tool in helping clients optimize their wealth.

Disability insurance can help your clients protect their wealth from knowable and unforeseen events by helping them:

▲ **Protect their standard of living from catastrophic events** by providing the assets needed to replace lost future income through **income replacement benefits.** This helps clients at best still realize all their goals and at worst maintain choice, dignity, and independence in times of great trial.

▲ **Ensure the family's ability to maintain their lifestyle** by protecting them from the life and socioeconomic displacement due to an "un-timely" disability through **income replacement benefits.**

▲ **Preserve freedom of choice** by protecting them from the significant reduction in quality of life caused by the loss of current and future income through **income replacement benefits.** This helps clients maintain their dignity and independence throughout their lives regardless of circumstance.

## LONG-TERM CARE INSURANCE

For an aging society, long-term care insurance is a critical tool in protecting a client's wealth from being decimated by a catastrophic illness.

Long-term care insurance can help protect wealth from knowable and unforeseen events by helping clients:

▲ Make appropriate investment decisions

▲ Gain the confidence to take action and stay invested

▲ Protect them from catastrophic events

▲ Ensure the family's ability to maintain their lifestyle

Long-term care provides help when you have a prolonged physical illness, disability, or cognitive impairment (such as Alzheimer's disease) that keeps you from living an independent lifestyle. These limitations may prevent you from carrying out basic self-care tasks, called Activities of Daily Living (ADLs). ADLs may include things such as bathing, dressing, or eating.

# LONG-TERM CARE INSURANCE KEY FEATURES

## Coverage

You can choose long-term care policies that pay only for nursing home care or only for homecare. Or, you can opt to purchase coverage for a mixture of care options that includes nursing home, assisted living, and adult day care. Some will pay for a family member or friend to care for you in your home.

## Daily or Monthly Benefit

The daily or monthly benefit is the amount of money the insurance company will pay for each day or month you are covered by a long-term care policy.

## Benefit Period

Your benefit period determines the length of time you will receive benefits from your policy. You can choose a benefit period that spans from two to six years, or the rest of your life.

## Elimination or Waiting Period

During this period, you must pay all of your long-term care expenses out of your own pocket. This period could last anywhere from 0 to 100 days. The longer the waiting period is, the lower your premiums will be.

## Inflation Protection

There are two main kinds of inflation protection: the right to add coverage at a later date and automatic coverage increases.

## Non-Forfeiture Benefit

Policies with this benefit will continue to pay for your care even if you stop paying premiums. This policy feature can add 10 percent to 100 percent to your premium.

## Indemnity Long Term Care Insurance Payment

Under this option, the long term care insurance company will send you a check for the policy's full daily or monthly benefit regardless if the actual expenses were less. If there is extra money left over than you can spend it anyway you see fit.

## Shared Benefit Coverage for Couples

This optional rider allows couples to share each other's benefits. If one spouse needs long-term care and runs out of money in their policy, they then can dip into their spouse's policy and start to use their benefits.

**Waiver of Premium**

When you need long-term care most of the top companies will waive your premium once you go on claim and start receiving benefit.

**Return of Premium Benefit**

This benefit is a rider that some companies offer that will return all or a portion of the long-term care insurance premiums paid back to your beneficiary at your death.

## LONG-TERM CARE INSURANCE FEES AND EXPENSES

**Premium**

This is the cost of actually having insurance protection. It is based on the insured person's age, gender, and health along with the benefit amount, benefit period and other optional features

## THE VALUE OF LONG TERM CARE INSURANCE

What can long-term care insurance do to help your clients optimize their wealth? What do your clients get for the premiums they pay?

**Long-term care insurance can help your clients protect their wealth from knowable and unforeseen events by helping them:**

▲ **Protect their wealth from catastrophic events** by providing the assets needed to fund long-term assistance through **LTC benefits.** This helps clients maintain choice, dignity and independence in times of great trial.

▲ **Ensure the family's ability to maintain their lifestyle** by protecting them from the life and socioeconomic displacement caused by the catastrophic expense associated with a long-term care through **LTC benefits.**

▲ **Preserve freedom of choice** by protecting them from the significant reduction in quality of life caused by the expense of a long-term illness through **LTC benefits.** This helps clients maintain choice, dignity and independence throughout their lives regardless of circumstance.

# ALTERNATIVE INVESTMENTS

Other useful investment vehicles include real estate investment trusts (REITs), commodities (gold, silver, etc.) and private placements. Alternative investments can be useful tools in helping your clients optimize their wealth.

**Alternative investments can protect their wealth from knowable and unforeseen events by helping clients:**

▲ Make appropriate investment decisions

▲ Gain the confidence to take action and stay invested

**Alternative investments can facilitate the growth potential of investible assets by helping clients:**

▲ Maximize investment diversification and efficiency

▲ Adapt their portfolios in response to changing market conditions and life events

A **real estate investment trust** is a security that sells like a stock on the major exchanges and invests in real estate directly, either through properties or mortgages. REITs receive special tax considerations and typically offer investors high yields, as well as a highly liquid method of investing in real estate.

Equity REITs: Equity REITs invest in and own properties (thus responsible for the equity or value of their real estate assets). Their revenues come principally from their properties' rents.

A **commodity** is anything for which there is demand, but which is supplied without qualitative differentiation across a market. Well-established physical commodities have actively traded spot and derivative markets. Generally, these are basic resources and agricultural products such as iron ore, crude oil, coal, ethanol, sugar, coffee beans, soybeans, aluminum, rice, wheat, gold and silver.

A **private placement** is the raising of capital via private rather than public placement. The result is the sale of securities to a relatively small number of investors. Since a private placement is offered to a few select individuals, the placement does not have to be registered with the Securities and Exchange Commission.

## KEY FEATURES OF ALTERNATIVE INVESTMENTS

**Professional Investment Management**
Full-time, high-level professional management is behind most

alternative investments with the managers' interests tied to consumers because their compensation is based on how well the "investment" performs.

The key feature of alternative investments is their ability to further diversify a client's portfolio and even hedge bear market conditions.

**Alternative Investments Fees and Expenses**
The expenses related to alternative investments do vary, yet are very similar to the fees and expenses of professionally managed money and usually include a **sales load, management fees and operating expense, 12b-1 fee and redemption fees**

## THE VALUE OF ALTERNATIVE INVESTMENTS

What can alternative investments do to help your clients optimize their wealth? What do your clients get for the fees and expenses they pay?

**Alternative investments can help your clients protect their wealth from knowable and unforeseen events by helping them:**

▲ **Make appropriate investment decisions** by providing effective investment guidance through **professional investment management.** This protects clients from the dangers inherent in over-weighted or miss-allocated portfolios .

▲ **Gain the confidence to take action and stay invested** by providing effective investment guidance through **professional investment management and diversification.** This helps to protect clients from the risks inherent in market fluctuations giving clients greater peace of mind with their investment relative to risk.

**Alternative investments can help your clients facilitate the growth potential of their investible assets by helping them:**

▲ **Maximize investment diversification and efficiency** by reducing the effect of volatility on the consistency of return relative to risk. This gives clients the opportunity to gain more consistent results and accumulate more assets over the long term.

▲ **Adapt their portfolios in response to changing market conditions** by ensuring a continual alignment between the world context/reality and their investment strategy through professional investment management and diversification. This gives clients the ability to maximize their investment strategy regardless of world events.

## DEEPENING YOUR KNOWLEDGE

As I said at the beginning of the chapter the greater your skill and the deeper your expertise in using the value inherent in the multitude of financial products available to you, the better you can serve your clients and help them achieve their financial and life goals. So the next step to being a true advisor and attracting more affluent clients is to become familiar with and gain a working knowledge of the products and services that you currently don't offer, the products and services outside your specialty or focus.

This starts by internalizing the value of each product from the preceding pages, learning the linkages between their features and their value, and then gaining a better understanding of the inner workings of each. Wholesalers can be great resources for helping you gain product expertise and to partner with in client meetings, as well as other FAs, so lean on both. Your goal is to know what a product does – its value – and enough about what it is to be conversant and confident in their use so you offer the comprehensive services that today's consumer is looking for.

### Advisor Commentary

**Being a financial advisor is a career that is requires continuous learning. It's part of our responsibility, and part of my ongoing preparation to best help my clients. I take advantage of every firm sponsored event and due diligence meeting. I tap into the expertise of colleagues and wholesalers and every learning experience that will help me do a better job at serving my clients. The resources are out there so use them.**

# CHAPTER SIX

# Practice 4 – Develop Highly Effective Strategies

*Good plans shape good decisions. That's why good planning helps to make elusive dreams come true."*
– Lester R. Bittel

Knowledge is the first step to offering the comprehensive services consumers need; knowing the products and services available and understanding the value they offer. The next key practice of the most successful in the industry is understanding how to apply that value strategically – how to leverage the value inherent in financial products and services to help each client optimize their wealth and realize their ideal life given the unique context of each. This is Practice 4 and the next point of divergence between the best and the rest.

PRODUCT VERSUS CLIENT-FOCUSED ADVISOR ATTRIBUTES

The strategies and deliverables of product-focused advisors are generally limited to their particular area of expertise. Product-focused advisors usually have little comfort outside their own specialty and hence rarely, if ever, offer products and services outside their own. Top advisors, on the other hand, employ a broad array of strategies and products to help clients optimize their wealth. Instead of shying away from the unknown, the best advisors seek out the value inherent in all available products and services and use whatever individual or combinations of products are needed to help clients move towards achieving their goals.

While having particular strategies and associated deliverables to overcome certain highly relevant issues that affluent consumers face, top advisors recognize that strategic success is by its nature conditional and focus on constructing strategies specific to the unique needs and situation of each client.

WEALTH OPTIMIZATION STRATEGY DEVELOPMENT

To help you construct wealth optimization plans unique to the needs of each client, here are four steps to developing effective strategies, plans of action to remove the barriers impeding the client's ability to move towards achieving their goals as efficiently and effectively as possible.

1. **Gain an accurate understanding of the client's current situation, their goals and their picture of an ideal life.** This is, of course, the basis for being a true advisor – being focused on the client and gaining an intimate understanding of their world, knowing where they are, what's important to them, and where they want to go.

2. **Identify the barriers, obstacles, and issues keeping the client from optimizing their wealth and realizing their ideal future.** Ultimately, these barriers are revealed as the absence of the value you can offer. So all of the issues that consumers face – the primary obstacles to optimizing their wealth and realizing their ideal life – can be distilled down to the absence of one or more of the value attributes (from Practice 2) that a financial advisor can offer.

3. **Determine which products or services deliver the value needed to help clients optimize their wealth, to fill the void caused by the absence of value.** In many cases more then one "tool" (product or service) will possess the value attributes the client needs to best achieve their financial and life goals.

4. **Construct the most efficient and effective mix of products and services for the client's unique needs and circumstances.** Find the best combination of products and services based on your client's unique situation.

## UNDERSTANDING YOUR CLIENTS

Crafting effective wealth optimization strategies is predicated on your knowledge of the client and their world. Without good intelligence effective strategic design is merely blind luck, like trying to drive somewhere without knowing where you are or where you're going. Because of this uncovering the "truth" about a client's life, their goals and dreams is critical.

Two kinds of questions that are useful in getting the information you need to develop an effective strategy are goal questions, which uncover what is really important to a client and gap questions which reveal a client's current financial picture and plan. Here are some examples. We'll explore the process of *inquiry* in more detail in Chapter Nine.

### Financial Goals

What are your financial goals?

How do you determine the success of an investment?

### Life Goals

What's important to you?

Who in your life do you care about most?

What are three goals you have yet to accomplish in your life?

If you didn't have to work anymore, what would you do?

### Retirement Goals

When do you want to retire?

What is your picture of an ideal retirement?

How much money would need to not worry about money?

### Legacy Goals

What are your legacy goals?

How do you want people to remember you?

How do you measure a person's success in life?

What goals do you have for your loved ones?

### Gap Questions

What is your current financial picture? Income, outflow, retirement savings, cash, portfolio, debt, insurance?

Do you have a formal financial plan in place?

On a scale from 0 to 10, how much confidence do you have in your financial plan?

What do you think may happen to your financial picture over the next year, over the next five years?

What are you not getting from your financial advisor?

What would you like to be doing better financially?

What's getting in the way of optimizing your wealth?

What are your key concerns about realizing your goals?

Here's a simple work through of the wealth optimization strategy development process using two relevant themes, *Preparing for Retirement in Uncertain World* and *Maximizing Ones Legacy*, to help you better understand how the process works.

## PREPARING FOR RETIREMENT IN AN UNCERTAIN WORLD

### STEP 1 – Understand the Client

#### Client Goals

**Retirement** – Have financial freedom to enjoy their desired lifestyle with both confidence and certainty

**Financial** – Fund desired lifestyle and maintain independence until the end

**Life** – Age 55, desire to retire at 60, travel, community involvement

**Legacy** – enjoy entire life on their terms, no burden, and fund grandchildren's and great grand children's college education

#### Current Situation

Large portion of investable assets in money market due to current political, economic, and world environment

Tends to jump in and out of market

Needs growth to fund lifestyle goal

$3 million in assets, owns home, $250k net income,

$2 million in life insurance with $300k in cash value in a 15-year-old policy

Maxes out all qualified investments with conservative allocation

### STEP 2 – Identify the key barriers to optimizing wealth

▲ The client isn't making appropriate investment decisions or maximizing investment diversification and efficiency. Needs growth to fund lifestyle yet current risk tolerance is conservative due to political and economic climate – fear of losing money in a volatile market

▲ The client isn't taking action and staying invested, frequently changes course with investments and is reducing returns because of it

▲ The client doesn't know if they'll outlive their wealth creating uncertainty as to their ability to fund their desired lifestyle

▲ The client is not protected against debilitating illness or catastrophic events, putting the family at risk of losing the ability to maintain their lifestyle and freedom of choice

**STEP 3 – Determine the value needed to help the client optimize their wealth and the products that can deliver the value**

### THE CLIENT NEEDS TO BE PROTECTED FROM KNOW AND UNFORESEEN EVENTS AND

#### Make appropriate investment decision

**Mutual funds** – professional money management, asset allocation and dollar-cost-averaging

**Annuities** – living benefits

#### Gain the confidence to take action and stay invested

**Mutual funds** – professional money management, asset allocation

**Annuities** – living benefits

#### Protect against catastrophic events

**Long-term care** – LTC benefits

**Annuities** – living benefits

#### Help ensure the family's ability to maintain their lifestyle

**Long-term care** – LTC benefits

#### Preserve freedom of choice

**Annuities** – annuitization and living benefits

**Long-term care** – LTC benefits

## THE CLIENT NEEDS TO GROW THEIR
## INVESTIBLE ASSETS AND:

### Control the timing and impact of their tax burden

**Qualified plans** – tax deferral

**Annuities** – tax deferral

**Life insurance** – tax advantaged

### Have well-chosen investment selections regardless of risk

**Mutual funds** – professional money management across the risk spectrum

### Maximize investment diversification and efficiency

**Mutual funds** – asset allocation, professional money management

**Annuities** – tax deferral

### Adapt their portfolios in response to changing market conditions and life events

**Mutual funds** – professional money management across all sectors

### Utilize alternative strategies for retirement income

**Annuities** – tax deferral, living benefits, annuitization, professional money management, diversification, and dollar cost averaging

**Life Insurance** – tax advantaged growth and income, professional money management, diversification, and dollar cost averaging

## THE CLIENT NEEDS TO BE ABLE TO EFFECTIVELY DRAW
## UPON AND UTILIZE THEIR ASSETS AND:

### Have multiple income options and flexible payouts

**Annuities** – annuitization, living benefits

**Life Insurance** – tax advantaged income

### Provide an opportunity to create predictable lifetime income

**Annuities** – annuitization, living benefits

STEP 4 – Construct the most efficient and effective mix of products and services for the client's unique needs and circumstances.

Here is a sample (the numbers are for demonstration purposes only) to help this particular client achieve their goals – live their desired lifestyle, maintain independence and choice until the end, and fund the college education of their grandchildren and great grandchildren.

▲ **Continue maxing contribution to qualified accounts using mutual funds with asset allocation. This will help the client:**

*Control the timing and impact of the tax burden* by accelerating growth and minimizing taxes on income through **tax deferral.**

*Make appropriate investment decisions* by leveraging the knowledge and expertise of **professional money management** and by using **asset allocation** models.

*Maximize investment diversification and efficiency* through **professional money management** and **asset allocation.**

*Gain the confidence to take action and stay invested* through the trust engendered by historic success of long-term well diversified **professionally managed investments.**

▲ **Allocate 20 % of investable assets into a variable annuity with a living benefit. This will help the client:**

*Make appropriate investment decisions and gain the confidence to take action and stay invested* by removing the downside affects of market volatility through **living benefits, professional money management** and **asset allocation.**

*Control the timing and impact of the tax burden* by accelerating growth and minimizing taxes on income through **tax deferral.**

*Maximize investment diversification and efficiency* through of **professional money management** and **asset allocation.**

*Leverage an alternative strategy for retirement income* through **tax deferral, professional money management, living benefits** and **annuitization.**

*Protect against catastrophic events* by protecting principle and even market gains from market losses at times of withdrawal through **living benefits.**

*Have the comfort to know that they will never outlive their income and preserve freedom of choice* by providing guaranteed retirement income regardless of market performance through **annuitization** and **living benefits.**

▲ **Allocate 50% of investible assets into proven and steady mutual funds. This will help the client:**

*Make appropriate investment decisions and gain the confidence to take action and stay invested* by leveraging proven knowledge and expertise of **professional money management.**

*Maximize investment diversification and efficiency* through **professional money management and asset allocation.**

*Provide well-chosen investment selections regardless of risk* through **professional money management** across the risk spectrum.

▲ **Purchase Long-term Care Insurance. This will help the client:**

*Protect themselves from catastrophic events* by providing the assets needed to fund long-term assistance through **LTC benefits.** This helps clients maintain choice, dignity and independence in times of greater trial.

*Help ensure the family's ability to maintain their lifestyle* by protecting them from the life and socioeconomic displacement caused by the personal and monetary price associated with providing long-term care through **LTC benefits.**

*Preserve freedom of choice* by protecting them from the significant reduction in quality of life caused by chronic illness through **LTC benefits.** This helps clients maintain choice, dignity, and independence throughout their lives regardless of circumstance.

▲ **Purchase variable life insurance policy with cash value from old policy and contribute maximum amount until retirement. This will help the client:**

*Leverage an alternative strategy for retirement income* through **tax advantaged growth and income and professional money management.**

*Control the timing and impact of the tax burden* by accelerating growth and minimizing taxes on income through **tax advantaged growth and income.**

*Enjoy their wealth without jeopardizing their legacy* and help clients realize their ideal life and desired legacy by letting them spend their wealth in their lifetime, enjoying the fruits of it, and still pass on wealth to future generations or important causes through **tax-free death benefits.**

## MAXIMIZING ONES LEGACY

### STEP 1 – Understand the Client

*Clients Goals*

**Retirement** – travel and live in own home until the end

**Legacy** – wants to pass on as much of self-made wealth to heirs, children and grandchildren, along with values and work ethic that created the wealth

*Current Situation*

$43 million in wealth, $20 million in family heirloom asset

Conservative investments

Living desired lifestyle without touching principle

Good health

Self-insured

Concerned about heirs mishandling wealth

### STEP 2 – Identify the key barriers to optimizing wealth

▲ The client isn't set up to transfer wealth in a tax efficient manner keeping them from passing as much as they can to family and foundations.

▲ The client doesn't have the liquid capital needed to offset potential tax burdens without exhausting their liquid wealth or liquidating their family heirloom.

▲ The client can't be assured that the values, integrity, and work ethic that created the wealth will be passed on to future generations.

**STEP 3 – Determine the value needed to help the client optimize their wealth and the products that can deliver it**

### THE CLIENT NEEDS HELP TO EFFECTIVELY DISTRIBUTE THEIR WEALTH FROM ONE GENERATION TO THE NEXT

**Transfer wealth in a tax efficient manner**

Life insurance – tax free, probate free death benefit

**Create need liquid capital to offset potential tax burdens**

Life insurance – death benefit

**Transfer the value, integrity, and work ethic to future generations**

Life insurance trust – control

**STEP 4 – Construct the most efficient and effective mix for the client's unique needs and circumstances.**

Here is a sample strategy to help the client achieve their legacy goal and pass as much of their wealth on along with their values and work ethic.

▲ Purchase $25 million (face amount) of single premium life insurance. This will help the client:

*Transfer their wealth in a tax efficient manner* by minimizing the effect of taxes on inter-generational transfer through **death benefits,** helping clients maximize their legacy.

*Create liquid capital needed to offset potential tax burdens* by protecting against a reduction in liquid assets or through **death benefits.** This allows clients to avoid the liquidation of "family heirloom" assets.

▲ Create an Irrevocable Life Insurance Trust and place the life insurance in the trust. This will help the client:

*Transfer their value, integrity, and work ethic to future generations* through an **irrevocable life insurance trust** and ensure the values that made them successful will do the same for their next generation and beyond.

These are just two examples of how the wealth optimization strategy development process works. Ultimately developing powerful wealth optimization strategies takes both rigor and repetition – the disciplined and persistent application of the strategic planning process. Effective wealth optimization strategies are the architecture for helping clients realize their financial, life, retirement, and legacy goals. Made transparent the strategy development process also gives clients a clear understanding of what they're doing and why they're doing it. There is a sound process behind the plan and this gives clients greater confidence in the financial plan and in you.

*It is process that gives meaning to life and meaning is the core of life*

## BROADEN YOUR CAPACITY

Offering the comprehensive services that affluent consumers both want and need requires in-depth knowledge of the financial products available to you and the value of each, combined with the ability to craft effective wealth optimization strategies unique to each client. This knowledge and strategic acumen, or more importantly the outcome of their application, is at the core of what top advisors do for their clients. The implementation of effective wealth optimization strategies using a broad base of products is what the best deliver and how they help their clients succeed. So to attract more affluent clients you need to do the same thing – offering more holistic and comprehensive services. For some this could mean earning advanced designations and for others it might mean aggressively partnering with other complementary specialist, or both, or somewhere in between.  But ultimately if you want to move up market it means building your capacity to offer the comprehensive services that affluent consumers are looking for.

OFFERING COMPREHENSIVE SERVICES

## Practice 3 – Have In-Depth Knowledge of Financial Planning

Understanding all of the financial products (tools) available to you is the first step to offering the comprehensive services today's consumer needs. Use the following to determine what you need to learn more about and who can help you.

**For each of the following products:**

**1– Describe what they can do, the value they offer for consumers**

**2– Note applications that might be particularly relevant for your market**

**3– Determine your proficiency, what you know well and where you need to learn more**

**4– Identify those you can partner with to learn more**

**Annuities**

Value:

Applications:

Proficiency:

Partners:

## Life Insurance

Value:

Applications:

Proficiency:

Partners:

## Professionally Managed Money

Value:

Applications:


Proficiency:


Partners:


## Long-Term Care

Value:


Applications:


Proficiency:


Partners:

## Disability Insurance

Value:

Applications:

Proficiency:

Partners:

## Alternative Investments

Value:

Applications:

Proficiency:


Partners:



Finally what is your overall learning strategy to gaining an in-depth knowledge of all available financial products and tools?

**Practice 4 – Develop with Highly Effective Strategies**

Strategic thinking is the basis for effective financial planning. Creating effective strategies is a process fueled by knowledge of the value you have to offer and of the client's unique situation and life.

**How rigorous is your strategic thinking?**

Reflecting on your current clients answer the following questions.

1. How well do you understand their current situation, their goals and picture of ideal life?

2. Have you clearly identified the barriers, obstacles, and issues "in the way" of the client optimizing their wealth and realizing their ideal future.

3. Did you consider all available products that offer the value needed by your clients.

4. Did you utilize the most efficient and effective mix of product for your clients unique needs and circumstances.

How well do you know your clients, their lives, goals, and the barriers to optimizing their wealth? Which clients to you want or need to learn more about?

Are there opportunities to create more effective wealth optimization strategies for your clients? Which clients would benefit from a more comprehensive and effective financial strategy?

# My Plan For Offering Comprehensive Services

# Maximize Your Market Impact

SECTION FOUR looks at Practice 5 and how top advisors are able to optimize their own success and that of those they serve by effectively reaching their market and fully leveraging their value.

**PRACTICE 5**

Utilize High Performance Business Processes

CHAPTER SEVEN reviews the advanced business processes – strategic planning, branding, marketing, innovation, partnering and metrics – that will help you maximize your market impact and your practice success.

SECTION

4

# Practice 5:
## Utilize High Performance Business Processes

So far we've explored the foundational components of a great advisory practice, the basis for being the kind of financial advisor that affluent consumers are attracted to. You know what it means to embrace a client-focused strategy. You understand the value you bring to the market and how to broaden your offerings to serve the comprehensive needs of today's consumer. The next step to achieving top producer success is to propagate your value, to employ the high performance business processes that will allow you to effectively reach and efficiently serve your target market and ultimately maximize your market impact. This is Practice 5 and the next point of divergence between top producers and the rest.

> *"Knowledge is Power*
>
> *–Sir Francis Bacon*

### PRODUCT VERSUS CLIENT-FOCUSED ADVISOR ATTRIBUTES

Because of their goals and orientation product-focused advisors tend to run sales practices and use processes that often revolve solely around client interaction and selling techniques such as prospecting, qualifying, questioning, and closing. Conversely the most successful in the industry run high performance advisory practices with the primary goal of fulfilling. They use processes that enable them to fully leverage the value they have to offer to the benefit of their clients and to themselves. While excelling at the art of client engagement (Practice 7) top advisors also leverage advanced strategic planning, branding, marketing, innovation, partnering, and metrics to ensure they reach their target market and deliver their services as efficiently and effectively as possible.

> *Propagate – to spread (a report, doctrine, practice, etc.) from person to person; to disseminate. Origin: 1560–70; from pangere and propāgātus (Latin) - to fasten and to spread for sprouting.*

Here are some core principles and processes from each discipline that will help you run a higher performance practice.

## STRATEGIC PLANNING

We've already talked about how to create effective wealth optimization strategies in the last chapter and fundamentally this book is about strategy, thoughtful planning designed to achieve particular outcomes. There are five primary levels of strategic thinking that are useful to financial advisors.

1. Enterprise-wide positioning strategies to capture broad market opportunities

2. Target market competitive strategies to differentiate yourself from competitors and gain new clients

3. Wealth optimization strategies to help your clients optimize their wealth

4. Operational efficiency strategies to optimize internal work process flow and efficiency

5. Personal development strategies to realize learning and professional development goals

## THE STRATEGY DEVELOPMENT PROCESS

To most people strategic planning is the act of planning for a certain outcome; if you do A and B, you can be certain that C will happen. The idea that we can predict what will happen with certainty is born from the sciences of the 1700s; Newton's law of gravity is a perfect example. Yet the same body of knowledge – physics – that proves with certainty that if you drop an apple from a tree it will fall to the ground also reveals that it is impossible to know with certainty the future outcomes of events before they occur (Heisenberg's Uncertainty Principle) and that future outcomes are highly sensitive to small changes in the initial conditions (Chaos Theory). This means forward planning in the framework of 21st century science isn't about certainty but instead about probabilities. Strategic planning isn't about

### Advisor Commentary

**We all know that having an investment process is important to be effective in helping our clients yet we believe it is just as important to have processes to help us run an effective business. Each of the following disciplines is key to our success and important to yours as well.**

constructing rigid plans but instead it's about crafting flexible strategies that can adapt to changing dynamics as they arise, to identify possible future scenarios and consider what the best approach would be in each.

> *process - a systematic series of actions directed to some end Origin: 1275–1325; from processus (Latin) – going forward*

Here are some key components to effective strategic thinking at all levels.

**Strategic Goal** – what do you want to accomplish, what opportunity to you want to capture, what threat do you want to protect against? Define key metrics to know when you've realized your desired future state or outcomes. Be specific and define indicators from multiple perspectives, yours, clients, market, etc.

**Strategic Assessment** – is the opportunity aligned with your purpose and values? What is the time horizon of the planning? How well did your strategy work last time you had a similar opportunity?

**Strategic Analysis** – what are the strategic challenges you face and advantages you possess in terms of your service model, operational issues, your people and culture? What additional skill or expertise is needed to achieve your strategic end?

**Strategic Action Plan** – What are your short and long-term action plans, with contingencies, that leverage your strengths and competitive advantages. What are the benchmarks that mark your progress towards the achievement of your strategic goal.

**Tactical Execution** – Who does what to execute the action plan.

**Performance Management** – How well is the strategy performing based on your defined metrics? Do you need to adjust your tactical and or strategic plans.

While having hope is important just remember that hope, on it's own, is not an effective strategy (I hope I get more clients, I hope I earn more money) so be diligent in your strategic thinking and use it to leverage your value to the fullest extent. .

## BRANDING

Effective branding is another key driver of advisor success. Your brand is defined through the eyes of your clients, your target market and other stakeholders; it is the collective perception of you, by the world around you. Creating and publicizing a high value, high performance brand is at the root of top advisor success. To help you better understand how you can create and leverage a strong brand Colin Bates offers some insight from his book *How to Build Your Total Brand.*

> *"Your premium brand had better be delivering something special, or it's not going to get the buisiness"*
> – *Warren Buffet*

## Advisor Commentary

Just as we use strategic thinking to craft our client's financial plans, we do the same in running our business. We think strategically when creating our business plan, in our marketing efforts and in our internal operations. The whole point of all of our planning is to create the best client experience possible as we know this is what ultimately drives our success. Everything we think about is how to make it better for our clients especially in the world today. One example of our strategic planning is our morning meeting; every morning our team gets together for 10 minutes, we talk about strategy for the day, what each team member/department can do to make life easier for the clients we are engaging with and focused on that day. I want everyone in the room to weigh in regardless of their role. Traditionally the advisor meets with the client and then hands off "to do's" to the sales assistant. But giving some thoughtful discussion, whether it's between you and a fellow FA, you and your assistant, or you and your team about what you can do to make your interactions that day a great experience for your clients and prospective clients is critical. For us every day starts with sitting down and saying here's the client and situation, what do we need and what can we do to make it a great experience and generate the best possible outcome for them? It's forward thinking before they walk in and the cornerstone of our success.

# THE PRINCIPLES OF BRAND MANAGEMENT
## (edited excerpts)

Here are five of the principles Bates offers for successful brand management. They form the basis for the 'principled decision making' needed to ensure brand success.

1. Brand value is built in the minds of customers and stakeholders

2. Brands are built through everything that you do, say and are

3. Brands are built through consistency over time

4. Always think, and talk, in terms of your current and desired brand

5. A corporate brand can be the driving force for an entire business

### Brand value is built in the minds of stakeholders

A brand is very different from a product or service. A brand is intangible; it exists in the mind of the customer.

### Brands are built through everything that you do, say and are

It is not just what you say that creates perceptions, far more important is what you do and what you are. Or, put another way: communications can play a role, but people trust their experiences much more.

Every business activity – from product development to sales and service – must fulfill its individual role within your business operations. But these activities must also contribute to the 'collection of perceptions' that you wish to build. They must work together to deliver a consistent message.

### Brands are built through consistency over time

It is no accident that many of the most valuable brands are also the oldest brands in the category or market. The reasons for this are two-fold:

First, it takes time to build a brand. There are some notable exceptions, but building the relationship between stakeholders and the brand usually takes considerable time. Confidence and trust grow slowly, and the simple longevity of the relationship adds to its strength, just like any other relationship.

Secondly, longevity can amplify the benefits of the brand. A long and rich heritage can help transform the experience through the associations and memories that it creates.

Consistency doesn't mean that a brand should stay still; strong brands evolve over time, in a number of different ways:

• Visually: many brands retained the essence of their visual identity, but update it and keep it looking 'current' through careful and in some cases, frequent, redesigns.

• Product development: the product evolves to meet the opportunities of new technology, changing consumer attitudes and other market developments.

• Fundamental promise: the essence of the brand, its fundamental promise, may also evolve in response to changing market dynamics.

**A corporate brand can be the driving force for the entire business**

Your brand is not just of value to your customers – a strong brand can also transform the behavior of all stakeholders. For example, strong brands can be clear guides to desired behavior and a source of inspiration.

Ultimately your brand, the markets perception of you and your value, is at the core of attracting more affluent clients.

## MARKETING

Advisors often only think about marketing in the context of target marketing, referral programs, seminars, client appreciation events and co-op advertising. While these tactics are part of any successful marketing program, high performance marketing goes beyond target marketing and prospecting techniques to include attention to the other elements that contribute to the successful marketing of your practice.

Marketing is the management and execution of the mix of product, pricing, promotion and packaging with the goal of fulfilling consumer demands and maximizing company profitability. Ultimately marketing is about attracting prospective clients, helping prospective

Your brand is your reputation and it takes a career to build and a moment to destroy. We've worked very hard to build our brand, a reputation for integrity and a great client experience. Through what we do and what we are, we have been successful in building a brand as trusted go to financial advisors. We recognize that anyone we partner with is part of our brand and will influence our markets perception of us, so we choose our partners carefully, with our staff as well as other FA's and wholesalers.

Your brand is communicated in every thing you do, your focus of attention, how you interact with clients, how you run your office, how you answer the phone, and how you conduct yourself when serving in the community. A brand of service excellence is key to attracting high net worth clients because it's what they are used to, they're familiar with and expecting Ritz Carlton quality of service. The high net worth client is generally more sophisticated and that's what they expect from their financial advisor. You have to be able to understand and live in their world. Ultimately it's about giving and exuding what the more affluent expect, demand, and deserve.

clients become clients, and helping clients become loyal clients. So while a key component of marketing is to attract the attention of the clients you want through seminars, referral programs, and other prospecting techniques it's ultimately about the client experience you create through the effective mix and congruence of the 4 Ps, product, pricing, promotion, and packaging.

*Congruence - agreement, harmony, conformity, or correspondence. Origin: 1400–50; from congruentia (Latin) to come together*

## Product

At the core of effective marketing is an outstanding product, something people want and need.

That's what this book is about, developing outstanding financial advisors able to help clients optimize their wealth and realize their ideal life, something affluent consumers want and need. Ultimately the outcome of your presence (your skill, expertise and strategies) – *the success realized by your clients* – is your product.

## Pricing

Whether you are fee based, commission based or both your price – the expense of your services – plays a big role in your ability to attract more affluent clients. If your clients or prospective clients think you're expensive – your price exceeds your value – they'll be less likley to engage your services, one of the reasons why it's so important to effectively convey your value. (Which we'll explore in the next chapter – Practice 6).

On the other end of the continuum it's important not to under price your services as people also attribute lower value to things with a lower price. Ultimately pricing is about finding a fair and equitable exchange that satisfies both parties; you deliver services considered worth the cost by your clients and you receive compensation you feel is worthwhile for the value you deliver.

## Promotion

This is what many advisors think about when they think marketing – "What can I do to promote myself and get more prospects in the door?" This, of course, is a critical component of an effective marketing effort. Yet keep in mind that without a great product, equitable pricing, and sharp packaging, promotion is an uphill battle. There are a numerous methods to promote your practice including referral programs, client and value-focused seminars, community involvement (civic marketing), and through the media – advertising, articles, columns, books, radio or TV. A key goal of any promotional activity is to convey the value you have to offer in way that entices your prospective clients to engage with you or at least be receptive to your approach.

## Packaging

This puts the proverbial box around the value you have to offer. Like the blue tiffany box, packaging does matter. The way you package and deliver your value has a distinct effect on the client experience and their satisfaction. Effective packaging, to start, needs to be congruent with the other 3 Ps and your brand (which are all inherently intertwined). Conveying real value through your packaging, the look, feel, and experience of your services, means attention to; 1- what people see, your appearance, yourself, your partners, your surroundings, your web presence; 2– what people touch, your office, your collateral materials, business cards, capabilities brochures, proposals; and 3– what people experience, your client engagement process, your people, the vibe, the outcomes.

### Advisor Commentary

Referrals are the lifeblood of a great advisory practice. While our clients tend to ask us early on what they can do for us, we don't ask for referrals right away. Instead we work to earn their trust over time with the goal of developing true advocates, to have our passion for them result in their passion for us. When our clients are talking with friends and or colleagues and the conversation turns to financial advisors we want them, because of their belief in what we do, to want to promote our practice and services. This really works. Our goal is not to get referrals, but instead to develop client relationship that generate referrals time and time again.

Ultimately successfully marketing your practice, maximizing your reach and attraction to your market requires attention to and congruence with all the 4 Ps.

## INNOVATION

Innovation, doing something new or different, is of course what this book is all about, and a skill critical to the success of advisors all along the value continuum. Innovation requires a healthy dose of curiosity, a real desire to be better, and the willingness to change.

Innovation isn't something you can plan with precision, instead innovation tends to emerge, sometimes on purpose yet many times when you least expect it. Many great discoveries have happened by accident – the laser, the integrated circuit and 3M post-it notes are examples. So while explicit efforts to innovate through targeted brainstorming sessions can be productive, innovation is best aided by creating a fertile environment for innovation to emerge.

The following steps can help you spur effective innovation.

1. Create an environment conducive to innovative thinking, a culture that rewards outside the box perspectives, challenging the status quo and a thirst for improvement.

2. Have an organizational design that allows for high levels of interaction and collaboration and actively looks for opportunities to improve.

3. Capture potentially valid and useful innovations as they emerge.

4. Experiment with potentially valid and useful innovations, just because it's different doesn't make it better. Determine if they are valid, as they are or with modifications, and worthy of adoption.

5. Culturally integrate the new practice, i.e. reward and expect its use.

Again innovation is at the core of this book and some argue that it's the only way to maintain a true competitive advantage.

## PARTNERING

The true concept of a partnership, a meaningful business partnership, often gets overlooked in the financial services industry. Whether between advisors and their clients or between advisors and other "professionals", relationships are often fleeting with little lasting value. In contrast meaningful and productive partnerships are built on an equitable and desirable exchange of value, with both parties bringing something of value to the other and in the process improving the level of success, the quality of life, of both.

Another place many FAs miss the mark is in innovation. In our practice we seek to learn from everyone and continually improve on what we do through professional development programs, firm sponsored educational opportunities, and meeting with wholesalers (we attend every wholesaler lunch and learn). Ultimately we model our business after law and medical practices, both of which require continuous learning to stay up to date (and even compliant).
We have a voracious appetite for learning and innovation because it is in the best interest of our clients and to prevent ourselves from becoming marginalized or commoditized, like so many advisors today.

The good news is since you are reading this book, you are innovating and ahead of the curve, open to growth, and wherever you are in your career cycle you are making the effort to stay responsibly connected to the information of the day. You're doing your job.

---

Key partners include clients, internal colleagues and staff, wholesalers, complimentary advisors, and other professional service providers that you work with.

Great partnerships don't happen by accident. They are the result of a purposeful intent. Here are the five steps to creating productive partnerships.

1. Identify your ideal partner attributes - what kind of people do you want to partner with? What value should they possess? What values should they operate by? What work styles are important to you?

2. Define the purpose of the partnership – why are you partnering? What's the value to both parties? What are the expected outcomes?

3. Gain an explicit partnership agreement – gain a mutual understanding of the purpose of the partnership, duration, ground rules, and clearly articulated responsibilities. Communication is key to a successful partnership – be explicit and don't let things go unsaid.

4. Perform as agreed upon – planning is important but the ultimate success of a partnership is dependant upon the execution of the agreed upon responsibilities.

5. Communicate continuously – continuous communication is critical to the success of any partnership. It is the conduit to ensure that roles are being fulfilled to the satisfaction of each partner, and so the partnership can adjust and even redefine itself relative to changing dynamics and needs.

Productive and meaningful partnerships are at the core of what top advisors do to be successful, with other professionals to increase the value they have to offer and with their clients to help them realize their financial and life goals.

## Advisor Commentary

We take our partnerships very seriously with our clients, our staff, and the wholesalers we work with. With our clients we want to partner with people that want and need our help. Regardless of the assets in play we're not interested in working with clients that aren't interested in working with us. We have a similar philosophy in selecting our staff. There are people that are looking for a job and there are people that are looking to serve and we want people who are looking for more then just a job. We hire people who want to and can make a difference.

While we depend on references and good referrals, the first step we take to determine if someone is appropriate to partner with is to just be quiet, let them talk and then listen. An individual's character and focus are usually revealed through their past experiences and character really matters to us. I'll ask a potential staff member to describe a challenging situation they had in a previous role, how they were involved, how they reacted and what was the final outcome. We're looking for examples of commitment, a willingness to explore all options and a desire to put the client first.

# METRICS

What you measure and what you are measured on greatly influences what you do. Metrics act as guides, informing you as to what is going well and what is not, helping you redirect or solidify your strategies and activities. While the things that product-focused advisors measure are valid and important – activity, pipeline, closing ratio and of course production – fully leveraging the value you have requires focusing on a broader set of metrics. To start it means recognizing that production is not the ultimate metric; being aware that chasing production can lead to behaviors and activities that are far removed from the best interests of the consumer.

So what is the ultimate metric and what do you need to focus on? The ultimate metric for a value and client-focused business model is client success, the optimization of their wealth and the realization of their life and legacy goals and for you the advisor a highly successful and sustainable business. Realizing these goals requires focusing on more then activity and production (although still important measurements) and tracking metrics that include:

1. Net new assets

2. Your perceived value to your target market (brand strength)

3. Client satisfaction and loyalty

    a. Percentage of assets

    b. Quality and frequency of referrals

    c. Responsiveness

    d. Inter-generational retention

4. Strategic effectiveness at all five levels

    a. Enterprise-wide positioning strategies

    b. Target market competitive strategies

    c. Wealth optimization strategies

    d. Operational efficiency strategies

    e. Personal development strategies

Using advanced metrics and creating a more comprehensive dashboard of success indicators ultimately gives you a greater understanding of the effectiveness, sustainability and ultimate success of your practice.

## FINALLY

This has just been a brief look at the business processes that help top advisors run high performance advisory practices, each a powerful tool in helping you maximize your market impact. Your ability to impact the success of your clients, to have a positive affect on the lives of those you work with is based not only on your capacity to create value but also on how well you can distribute your value. Mastering the art and science of strategic planning, branding, marketing, innovation, partnering and metrics is a critical step to ensuring that the value you have to offer reaches the market you serve.

# The Seven Practices Toolkit: Section Four

## UTILIZE HIGH PERFORMANCE BUSINESS PROCESSES

### Practice 5 – Maximizing Your Market Impact

High performance business processes are the critical to running highly efficient and productive advisory practices. How well are you performing with each of them? What can you do to get better? The following will help you determine your proficiency in these processes and explore ways to improve.

## STRATEGIC PLANNING

How well defined are your strategic plans, how rigorous is your strategic thinking? Review your current strategies using the following.

▲ **Enterprise-wide positioning strategies to capture broad market opportunities**

| | | |
|---|---|---|
| Defined Strategic Goals | YES ○ | NO ○ |
| Completed Strategic Assessment | YES ○ | NO ○ |
| Thorough Strategic Analysis | YES ○ | NO ○ |
| Well-Crafted Strategic Action Plan | YES ○ | NO ○ |
| Being Executed | YES ○ | NO ○ |
| Monitoring Performance Metrics | YES ○ | NO ○ |
| Adjusting Strategy as Needed | YES ○ | NO ○ |

▲ Target market competitive strategies to differentiate yourself from competitors and gain new clients

Defined Strategic Goals                     YES ○        NO ○

Completed Strategic Assessment              YES ○        NO ○

Thorough Strategic Analysis                 YES ○        NO ○

Well-Crafted Strategic Action Plan          YES ○        NO ○

Being Executed                              YES ○        NO ○

Monitoring Performance Metrics              YES ○        NO ○

Adjusting Strategy as Needed                YES ○        NO ○


▲ Wealth optimization strategies to help your clients realize their financial, life and retirement and legacy goals

Defined Strategic Goals                     YES ○        NO ○

Completed Strategic Assessment              YES ○        NO ○

Thorough Strategic Analysis                 YES ○        NO ○

Well-Crafted Strategic Action Plan          YES ○        NO ○

Being Executed                              YES ○        NO ○

Monitoring Performance Metrics              YES ○        NO ○

Adjusting Strategy as Needed                YES ○        NO ○

▲ Operational efficiency strategies to optimize internal work
   process flow and efficiency

| | | |
|---|---|---|
| Defined Strategic Goals | YES ○ | NO ○ |
| Completed Strategic Assessment | YES ○ | NO ○ |
| Thorough Strategic Analysis | YES ○ | NO ○ |
| Well-Crafted Strategic Action Plan | YES ○ | NO ○ |
| Being Executed | YES ○ | NO ○ |
| Monitoring Performance Metrics | YES ○ | NO ○ |
| Adjusting Strategy as Needed | YES ○ | NO ○ |

▲ Personal development strategies to realize learning and
   professional development goals

| | | |
|---|---|---|
| Defined Strategic Goals | YES ○ | NO ○ |
| Completed Strategic Assessment | YES ○ | NO ○ |
| Thorough Strategic Analysis | YES ○ | NO ○ |
| Well-Crafted Strategic Action Plan | YES ○ | NO ○ |
| Being Executed | YES ○ | NO ○ |
| Monitoring Performance Metrics | YES ○ | NO ○ |
| Adjusting Strategy as Needed | YES ○ | NO ○ |

# BRANDING

What is your current brand based on how you think you are perceived by your clients, your market and your community?

How does your presence, everything about you and your practice, contribute to your brand?

What do you want to change (or solidify) about your brand?

What do you need to do to change how your market perceives you?

What is your plan to institute the change?




## MARKETING

What client experience and ultimate outcome do you deliver?




Is it aligned with what more affluent consumers want?




What can you do to make the client experience and outcome better?

What is your pricing model and how do you explain it and justify it to clients?

What promotional activities could you add or enhance to increase your visibility and strengthen your brand with affluent consumers?

How are you packaged? Is it line with what the affluent expect?

What can you change about your packaging to better represent what the affluent want?

Ultimately how well are you leveraging the 4 Ps to meet consumer demands and maximize your success and sustainability?

What are you going to do differently?

## INNOVATION

Are you open to finding better (more optimal) ways of doing things?

Your firm?

Why?

What opportunities do you have to collaborate and discuss new ideas and concepts?

How can you create more of them?

PARTNERING

What are the ideal partner attributes for:

Clients:

Financial Advisors:

Wholesalers:

How well do your current partnerships align with your
ideal attributes?

How valuable are your current partnerships?

For you?

For your partners?

Which partnerships can you strengthen?

Which partnerships should you end?

## METRICS

What current measurements to you use to track the success
of your practice?


What additional metrics can you use to more accurately track you
practice success and sustainability?

# My Plan for Maximizing My Market Impact

# Be a True Advisor

PRACTICE 6
Convey Real Value

PRACTICE 7
Employ a
Consultative
Client-Focused
Approach

SECTION FIVE provides insight and guidance on employing Practices 6 & 7, the ability to convey real value and to employ a highly consultative client-focused advisory process, the crowning practices of the most successful financial advisors in the industry

CHAPTER EIGHT explores how the best in the industry effectively convey value through their words, actions and presence, in a way that resonates deeply with affluent consumers.

CHAPTER NINE looks at the inner workings of a consultative client-focused advisory process, the pinnacle practice of the best in the industry.

# Practice 6:
# Convey Real Value

To this point we've discussed the things top advisors do, how the best in the industry are of value to their clients. We've explored the client-focused strategy they embrace, the basis of their value, their knowledge and strategic acumen and their ability to reach and maximize their affect on their market. Ultimately you've learned how top producers build the capacity to attract more affluent clients.

> *"The least of things with a meaning is worth more in life than the greatest of things without it."*
> –Carl Jung

Now the focus shifts from *building your capacity* to be of value and *becoming a trusted advisor* to *leveraging your capacity* and *being a trusted advisor*. This takes us to the next practice and the first of the crowning practices shared by the industry's best – the ability to effectively convey value through words, actions and presence in a way that that resonates with affluent consumers. This is Practice 6 and the next point of divergence between the best and the rest.

## Advisor Commentary

Communication is the most vital component of a relationship, its like oxygen, whether communicating about something good, bad or just the status quo, all three forms of communication are important to building life-long relationships. The good is the easy part, it keeps people coming back and everybody does this. Communicating the status quo, reaching out when things are just going along and when times are bad is where most advisors fall short yet this is when clients need and want contact the most.

## PRODUCT VERSUS CLIENT-FOCUSED ADVISOR ATTRIBUTES

As we saw in Chapter Four, product-focused advisors generally define their value in terms of product expertise and product performance. Correspondingly their communication, actions, and presence are centered on product and performance, usually full of jargon and product detail. This translates into the number one thing consumers don't want, product complexity. Conversely top advisors define their value in how they help their clients realize their financial and life goals and convey value relevant to the client's world, their issues and needs.

We can't control markets but we can control our communication, so good, bad or the status quo, communicate. Particularly when times are bad, call clients in for a face to face. Let them vent and clear the air and explain the doom and gloom they feel. In doing so you'll most likely discover, beyond financial issues, what is really bothering them and often it's not the market or you but something else and this helps to the create the intimacy and emotional connection that develops clients for life.

*worldview – the framework of ideas and beliefs through which an individual interprets the world and interacts with it. Origin: 1855–60; translation of Weltanschauung (German)*

They communicate in away that resonates with the affluent consumer and effectively conveys the value of their advice and the value of the financial plans they put in place. The best exhibit value in everything they say, do and are and this, in large part, creates the attraction that draws the more affluent consumer to them.

## THE POWER OF SENSE MAKING

As we've already touched upon, a person's interpretation of what they see, read and hear is shaped by their unique worldview. This makes the process of knowing and understanding inherently personal and for anything to make sense to someone it needs to fall within his or her frame of reference. So your task is to do just that, convey value in a way that makes sense to your clients and prospective clients and fits within their frame of reference.

There are three ways you can convey value as a financial advisor. You can communicate the value of your client-focused strategy, your comprehensive services offerings, and your consultative approach through what you say – your words. You can express your capacity to help clients optimize their wealth through what you do – your actions. And you can convey your ability to help clients realize their ideal life and legacy through everything you are - your presence.

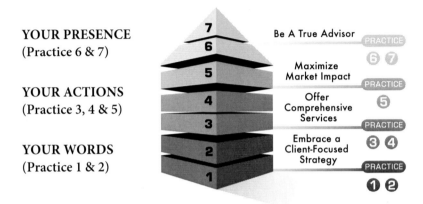

| YOUR PRESENCE (Practice 6 & 7) | | | |
| YOUR ACTIONS (Practice 3, 4 & 5) | | | |
| YOUR WORDS (Practice 1 & 2) | | | |

## COMMUNICATING VALUE THROUGH WHAT YOU SAY

**W**hat do you do? Not what are you, i.e., a broker, planner, or advisor but **what do you do? What is your purpose?** How you answer these questions is the first step to gaining the attention of more affluent clients. While product-focused advisors often reveal their self interests and singular focus when responding to these questions, top advisors effectively communicate the value of their client-focused practice model, the breadth and depth of their service offerings, and the consultative nature of their approach in a way that has meaning and value in the eyes of consumers.

Communicating your value starts with a great purpose statement, a concise and meaningful description of the value you bring to your clients. Stated with heartfelt sincerity and the belief in the value you offer, your purpose statement is the first step to attracting more affluent clients. Effectively answering the question "what do you do" and drilling down on "how you do it" in a way that is meaningful to consumers, requires a clear understanding of what they want and need to succeed (Practice 1) and real fluency in value-centric language (Practice 2).

One particular attribute of value-centric purpose statements and their client-focused explanations is their pull, their tendency to generate interest and the desire to learn more. Instead of saying very little in terms of meaning with a lot of words and disengaging people, often the nature of product-focused dialogue, value-centric purpose statements communicate a lot with few words, which leads to more questions. Questions like, "What do you mean by...?" "Would you tell me more about...?" "How do you...?" Which are all great questions for a prospect or client to ask.

Here are some examples of value-centric purpose statements with drill downs.

### What do you do? What's your value to me?

"What I do is work with clients (people, not unlike you) to help them optimize their wealth and realize their very important and intimate financial, life, retirement and legacy goals."

"I help my clients achieve their financial goals, get the most out of their money and ultimately realize their ideal life."

"My role is to help clients optimize their wealth so they can best realize their life and legacy goals."

"I'm a strategic partner to my clients in helping them get the most from their wealth, and realize their desired future however that is defined."

### How do you do it? What's you process?

"I do so through a comprehensive and consultative approach. It starts with gaining an intimate (a deep) understanding of my clients wants and needs, their financial and life goals, identifying the barriers to optimizing their wealth, and crafting strategies to help them best realize their financial and life goals all while simplifying what can be the complex process of financial planning."

"I help my clients optimize their wealth by providing strategies to; 1– protect their wealth from knowable and unforeseen events; 2– facilitate the growth of their investible assets, and; 3– effectively draw upon and distribute their wealth".

"I work closely with my clients, using a very consultative approach and often act as "quarterback" with their other advisors (accountant, lawyer, etc.) to put the plans in place to help them optimize their wealth (get the most life out of their money). I focus on three key areas; 1– protecting their wealth from knowable and unforeseen events; 2– facilitating the growth of their investible assets, and; 3– effectively drawing upon and distributing their wealth."

**What process/tools/products do you use to make all this happen?**

"I use a broad array of strategies and tools (products), whatever helps clients overcome the critical barriers that keep them from achieving their financial goals and realizing their ideal life"

"I use whatever strategies and tools (products) that help clients best achieve their financial goals and realize their ideal life."

"I offer the comprehensive services our clients ask for and need to help them navigate their unique path to realizing their ideal life and legacy. I use whatever strategies and products are best for each client's unique situation."

While this is a natural place to transition to questions (we'll talk more about that in the next chapter) you can also continue to describe in greater detail how you assist your clients by using the value-centric language from Practice 2.

You can also use value-centric language to construct capabilities presentations or as the basis for client-focused seminars. Here's an example of a value-centric capabilities presentation used as a component of a client-focused seminar.

*There is a big difference between knowing about something and knowing how something is done. Knowing about something is often superficial, while knowing how something is done is deep and inherently personal. The goal is to help your clients not only know about what you can do for them but to help them know how you do it, to understand what you do and how it relates to their world.*

## ▲ Introduction and agenda

"Thank you for taking the time to be here, we look forward to enjoying dinner with you tonight. Before we bring our speaker up and now that you've had a chance to settle in, have a glass of wine, let me spend a few minutes and share with you what we do. Our fundamental role is to help our clients optimize their wealth so they can best realize their life and legacy goals. We do so by **helping them protect their wealth from knowable and unforeseen events, facilitate the growth of their investible assets,** and finally by helping them **effectively draw upon and distribute their wealth.** Let me take a moment to touch on each."

## ▲ Protecting Wealth

"First we help our clients **protect their wealth from knowable and unforeseen events** as the health and prosperity of one's financial future is far from guaranteed."

"There are both market related events and personal risks, that can slowly erode or even decimate a person's ability to realize their life goals. To combat these events and offset the risks that threaten the optimization of wealth we help our clients **make appropriate investment decisions, gain the confidence to take action and stay invested and have the comfort to know that they will never outlive their income.** Doing this are just as much about protecting clients from themselves as it is protecting them from undue market risk."

"We also work with our clients to **protect their wealth from catastrophic events, ensure the family's ability to maintain their lifestyle, preserve freedom of choice, and retain the flexibility to continue transfer or sell business interests.** These things allow our clients to mitigate the risk associated with catastrophic health or market events."

"Ultimately we help our clients overcome the critical barriers to optimizing their wealth and realizing their life and legacy goals."

## ▲ Growing Wealth

"Because growing wealth is very important for most of our clients, as even the wealthiest want their money to grow so to pass it on to family, foundations and charities the next thing we do is to **help facilitate the growth of their investible assets.** We do this by helping clients **control the timing and impact of their tax burden, have well-chosen investment selections regardless of risk, maximize investment diversification and efficiency, adapt their portfolios in response to changing market conditions and life events and leverage alternative strategies for retirement income.** Ultimately we work to help our clients navigate the path to investment success."

▲   Drawing Upon Wealth

"Finally we help our clients **effectively draw upon and distribute their wealth,** This is the end game, the reason for the first two areas of focus, the ability to draw on wealth and to realize one's ideal life and to do so with confidence and certainty. We do this by helping our clients **have the choice of multiple income options and flexible income streams and the ability to create predictable lifetime income.** Doing this helps our clients realize their ideal life by removing uncertainty in future income, allowing them to focus on living the life they want with peace of mind."

"We also help our clients **enjoy their wealth without jeopardizing their legacy, enhance wealth through a leveraging effect, transfer wealth in a tax efficient manner, create need liquid capital to offset potential tax burdens and transfer their values, integrity, and work ethic to future generations.** Ultimately empowering our clients to realize their vision of an ideal future."

"So again the key areas we focus on are the **protection of wealth from knowable and unforeseen events,** helping our clients overcome the barriers to optimizing their wealth; the **growth of their investible assets,** helping them navigate the path to investment success; and finally to **effectively draw upon and distribute their wealth,** empowering our clients to realize their vision of an ideal future. Ultimately our role is to help our clients optimize their wealth so they can maximize their life and legacy"

"Of these three areas I've touched on which is most important to you?" This can be a rhetorical question or an actual poll and discussion around each of the areas, what people care about, what they do, and what they worry about most.

"If what I've shared is of interest and you want to learn more about how we might work together, indicate it on your feedback sheet or feel free to visit one of us before you leave."

"Now I want to introduce a speaker with a timely topic who will will give you more insight into [fill in with non-product, relevant and meaningful subject] while you begin to enjoy dinner"

## THE VALUE SANDWICH

When finally talking about product, the *value sandwich* is a useful method to help consumers understand why the product is of value and appropriate for them – what the product does in value-centric language – and the product's features and expenses – what the product is in product-centric language. It's called a value sandwich because you start and end with what the product does, it's value to the consumer, and in the middle describes what the product is. This reinforces and helps clients understand the most important thing, the value and affect of the strategy while still explaining the product(s) behind the strategy. Here are a few of examples:

### Annuity with a Living Benefit Rider

"What this strategy does is remove downside market risk and take the emotion out of investing helping you *make the right investment choices, take action and stay invested and to do so with comfort and confidence,* all critical steps to achieving your financial goals and in turn realizing your life and legacy goals."

"The tool that enables us to do this is a variable annuity with a living benefit rider. The variable annuity is an insurance product with an investment platform… The living benefit is an optional rider that provides a guaranteed minimum return on retirement income benefits… The costs are…"

"But again what this strategy does is help you remove the uncertainly of the market, *make appropriate investment decisions, take action and stay invested with real peace of mind,* all helping you realize your life and legacy goals."

## Mutual Funds

"What this strategy does is take the guesswork out of investing and reduce your exposure to market risk. It will help you *make appropriate investment decisions with confidence and maximize your investment diversification,* ultimately giving you the opportunity to gain more consistent long-term results and accumulate more assets."

"The strategy leverages a well-diversified portfolio with professional money management, effective asset allocation and dollar cost averaging investing. This means... The money managers I have in mind are... The holdings consist of... The cost are..."

"But again what this strategy does is to help *take the guesswork out of investing, reduce exposure to market risk and ultimately help you navigate the path to investment success.*"

## Life Insurance

"What this strategy does is allow you to *enjoy your wealth without jeopardizing your legacy or family heirloom assets. It will ensure that your values, integrity and work ethic will be passed on to future generations.*"

"The tool we use to make this happen is life insurance placed in a irrevocable life insurance trust... The life insurance will pay... This means... The trust will... This means... The costs are..."

"But again the core purpose of this strategy is to help *maximize your legacy while still letting you enjoy your wealth, to make sure that what you've worked a lifetime to build will last for generations to come.*"

Communicating value through your word is the first step to conveying real value. It helps you attract the attention of, generate interest from and get the clients you want. It's also the basis for simplifying the complex process of financial planning, the number one desire of today's consumer.

## EXPRESSING VALUE THROUGH YOUR ACTIONS

Building on the value you communicate, the next primary way to convey value is through what you do, turning your promise of value into action. Effectively expressing value through your actions starts with the sincere desire to help your clients and it's driven by your knowledge and strategic acumen.

Expressing value through your actions is not only about your financial planning acumen it's also about how you interact with your clients, your approach and process. It's based on your ability to gain an intimate understanding of your client's world and to help them fully grasp the reason for and the power of their financial plan, a plan designed to weather the cyclical nature of the market and best realize their financial goals. This is the essence of Practice 7, which we'll explore in the next chapter. Ultimately expressing value through your actions is based on your ability to craft and implement effective wealth optimization strategies that help your clients move towards achieving their financial and life goals.

## CONVEYING VALUE THROUGH YOUR PRESENCE

Presence is a powerful and sought after competency, it's an aura that emanates a distinctive quality, one that attracts positive interest and attention. Creating a powerful client-focused presence, the essence of what attracts more affluent clients, embodies everything this book is about – being of value and being highly professional in what you do.

Presence is defined at its core by who you are yet it's also impacted by everything about you that a client or market sees, hears, touches, and experiences. Your presence is your brand at a pheromone level as it's unspoken yet fills the room. Presence comes from the strong belief in the value you offer, combined with a strong dose of humility. Presence at its essence is humble confidence; true confidence in the value you have to offer and humble in the opportunity and responsibility to help others. Presence isn't about bragging about how great you are but instead it's about just doing great things and being thankful for the opportunity. A strong presence is something top advisors possess.

## FINALLY

Your ability to effectively convey value through what you say, what you do and ultimately who you are in a way that resonates with affluent consumers is important for you and the clients you serve. For you it's at the core of what attracts the more affluent client helping you build a more successful and sustainable practice. For your clients, it helps to satisfy their need to understand what they're doing and why they're doing it. This helps clients take action with confidence and stay the course, allowing them to generate better long-term results and ultimately realize their financial and life goals.

# CHAPTER NINE

# Practice 7: Employ a Consultative Client-Focused Advisory Process

> *Seek first to understand, then to be understood.*
>
> –Stephan Covey

We now come to the pinnacle practice shared by the best in the industry, a consultative client-focused advisory process that translates the top advisors' desire and capacity to help clients into meaningful and productive action. Through this value-centric advisory process top producers are able to effectively engage affluent prospects, uncover significant opportunities to bring real value and present strategies in a way that resonates with the client's world, issues, and needs helping them make highly informed decisions and take the action needed to best realize their financial and life goals. This is Practice 7, the ultimate point of divergence and differentiation between the best and the rest and the culminating practice that allows financial advisors to fulfill the role of "true advisor" and realize top producer success.

## PRODUCT VERSUS CLIENT-FOCUSED ADVISOR ATTRIBUTES

The core difference between product and client-focused advisors, and the attribute most discernable to the consumer, is the role they fill and the corresponding approach they use. Product-focused advisors, fundamentally, are salespeople and by nature are transactional in approach. In contrast client-focused advisors are more akin to professional service providers, they're not about selling but instead about fulfilling and as a result are highly consultative in nature. They are true professionals in their role as financial advisors.

> *Professional – a person who is expert at his or her work*
>
> *Advisor – someone who offers an opinion or recommendation as a guide to action, conduct, etc.*

How we interact with our clients is so important. When clients or prospects enter our office they are greeted with Ritz Carlton like hospitable and taken to our client education center, an area that's free of distractions. We let clients know that it is a "safe space" and that the meeting is about truly listening to them. We want to send a message that's this time is about them and to create a calm and inviting environment.

We start off our meetings by thanking them for taking the time to talk about something that is so important and for sharing it with us. We describe who are, what we do – our process – and how we help our clients. We paint a picture that they can relate to. Through our client discovery process we try to reveal ways we may or may not able to help them. We interview them and they interview us. The heart of the meeting is to discover what is truly important to them. Our job is to look at their current situation and life, their goals and their feeling and identify the disconnects that will keep them from achieving their goals. We let the client know that after the meeting we can mutually decide if it makes sense to work together. This gives the client control over the process as a client informed is a client in control. We find our most successful clients are the ones that are as equally engaged in the process as we are.

We let them know that we'll come back with one of three things; one, after our review we find they're OK, their advisor has done a great job; two, there are some disconnects but it's based on additional information they gave us that their existing advisor wasn't aware of, so will give them our recommendations to take back to their advisor to discuss; or three, we feel that we are the best choice to work with and we'll present our recommendation.

In presenting our strategy I try to keep it simple, to one page with bullet points. My goal is to take the *Wall Street Journal* reality and complexity and turn into story relating to the kitchen table.

## A CONSULTATIVE CLIENT-FOCUSED ADVISORY PROCESS

The goal of the client-focused advisory process is to help produce favorable outcomes – for everyone – by delivering the value needed to help clients optimize their wealth (get the most from their money) and best realize their life and legacy goals. Successfully employing a client-focused advisory process is based on proficiency and mastery of the first Six Practices – there are no shortcuts. If you are not committed to your clients' success or able to offer comprehensive services (or at least position your services within the wealth optimization model) than attempts to engage prospective clients will be fatally flawed as your self interests and or singular focus will be readily apparent.

Truly engaging clients and prospective clients starts with the environment you're in. The traditional across-the-desk set up is far from conducive to creating the connection needed for people to reveal what is personal and intimate to them. It's important to create a meeting space where everyone is on the same side of the table, at least figuratively, and that is inviting with no interruptions, no phone calls, emails, or computer screens. Your meeting space should convey your desired brand and be a place where people feel comfortable getting to know you and vice versa.

The client-focused advisory process is made up of four core steps and is a guide to getting from "hello, nice to meet you" to "thank you for your trust and the opportunity to be your financial advisor."

### A Meaningful Introduction

The purpose of a *meaningful introduction* is to gain the attention of and start to generate interest from your prospective client as well as set the direction of the meeting. The introduction is where you begin to establish credibility and plant the seeds of being trustworthy and useful.

### Effective Inquiry

*Effective inquiry* is the heart of the advisory process. The purpose of inquiry is to uncover the truth as to your prospects (or clients) life, goals and dreams along with a thorough and in-depth understanding of their financial picture. Effective inquiry requires both skill and tact.

## Strategy Development and Presentation

The purpose of the strategy development process and the presentation of the strategy is to turn your knowledge of the prospect, their current situation and their desired future into actionable strategies, then present those strategies so that the prospect clearly understands the why's and how's of the proposed actions. How you present your strategies is a critical step to helping prospects take the action needed to best realize their financial and life goals. Presenting your strategy effectively allows prospects to make highly informed decisions and be in control of the process.

## Gaining Commitment

Finally, the purpose of gaining commitment is to help people take action with both comfort and confidence, in the proposed plan and with you as an advisor. This is where you uncover and address any misunderstandings or barriers keeping clients from making decisions they fully understand and value.

## The Bridges

Bridges are critical linkages between each step of the advisory process. They allow you to naturally and effectively transition from one part of the process to the next. The bridges act to connect what has already been said and done with what is next, helping clients fully understand and be in full control of the advisory process. Let's take a closer look at each step.

## A Meaningful Introduction

You've finished the initial pleasantries and it's time to transition to business. What you say in the next 30 – 60 seconds will largely determine the extent to which the prospect will let you into their life; the extent that they will reveal the intimate details about themselves that you need to know to be of real value to them. How you articulate what you do and the reason for the meeting can and will make or break the opportunity. This is a critical point of differentiation; where salespeople often shut the prospect down by revealing their self-interests, true advisors begin to open the prospect up by demonstrating their credibility and client-focused agenda.

A meaningful introduction starts with your purpose statement and as discussed in the last chapter an effective purpose statement amongst other things conveys a great deal of value with few words. An effective purpose statement is a powerful mechanism that evokes interest from your audience and generates the desire to continue the conversation and explore what you might be able to do for them. A meaningful introduction is best delivered with conviction and sincerity and might go something like this.

"Thanks again for the time, let me start by sharing what I do, I know my card says financial advisor but let me tell you what that means. What I do is work with clients (people, not unlike you) to help them optimize their wealth and realize their very important and intimate financial, life, retirement and legacy goals"

"I do this by providing the strategies needed to 1) protect their wealth from knowable and unforeseen events, 2) to facilitate the growth of their investible assets, and 3) effectively draw upon and distribute their wealth in a way that allows them to realize their ideal life and legacy."

Or you can tailor it for a more specific client need.

"What I do is work with clients to help them optimize their wealth and realize their desired life and legacy. One area in particular is in helping clients transfer their values, integrity and work ethic along with their wealth to the next generation and beyond."

"I act as 'quarterback' with your other valued advisors (accountant, lawyer, etc.) to put the plans in place to help you maximize your legacy and its affect on future generations."

Regardless of the exact wording, the goal of your meaningful introduction is to convey value in a way that differentiates you from the masses and captures the attention of your prospect; to get them to them to recognize that your not just another "salesperson" trying to pitch a hot dot; for them to say "hmmm, I want to hear more" and be receptive to the questions you need to ask. A meaningful introduction also helps set the direction of the meeting and along with the bridge to inquiry, gain permission to move forward. This is where you begin to establish credibility and plant the seeds of being trustworthy and useful.

## THE BRIDGE TO INQUIRY

The bridge from your introduction to the process of inquiry is simple yet powerful in helping prospective clients open up to you. This bridge does three things. First it answers the prospect's unspoken question "why should I reveal anything about myself to this person?" Second, it acknowledges that being privy to information about their lives, particularly the personal and intimate information a financial advisor needs, is a privilege and not a right. Finally, the bridge gains permission to ask questions.

An effective bridge sounds something like this:

"In order to understand how I might be (or if I can be) of value to you, I need to ask you some questions, is that all right?"

Ultimately a meaningful introduction and an effective bridge helps you exhibit both purpose and professionalism. In the first 60 seconds, or less, they set you apart from the masses and allow you to effectively move into the next step of the advisory process.

All together it might go something like this:

"Thanks again for the time, let me start by sharing what I do, I know my card says financial advisor but let me tell you what that means. What I do is work with clients (people, not unlike you) to help them optimize their wealth and realize their very important and intimate financial, life, retirement and legacy goals."

"I do this by providing the strategies needed to; 1– protect their wealth from knowable and unforeseen events; 2– facilitate the growth of their investible assets and; 3– effectively draw upon and distribute their wealth in a way that allows them to realize their ideal life and legacy."

"In order to understand how I might be (or if I can be) of value to you, I need to ask you some questions, is that all right?"

## EFFECTIVE INQUIRY

The ultimate goal of effective inquiry – the process of revealing the truth – is to determine if and how you can be of value to a prospective client. In contrast to probing, which is about trying to find out how to position a product favorably so to sell more, effective inquiry is about understanding the truth about your clients and looking for situations where there is an absence of, and hence the need for, the value you offer.

Here are some basic principles that will help you find out the truth about your clients and prospective clients.

1.     Asking personal and even intimate questions is a privilege, not a right. So it's important to respect their privacy and ask for permission before venturing into their life.

2.     Have purpose and direction, know why you're asking the question and where you're going.

3.     Ask less invasive questions before moving on to more personal and intimate ones.

4.     Show respect and appreciation for their candor. You're being let in on what is important and personal, so be respectful and appreciative.

5.     Be truly curious.  Don't ask questions for the sake of asking questions; ask them because you're really curious about what they'll say. Don't assume you will know how they will answer.

6.     Listen intently. Don't be thinking about the next question you want to ask, focus instead on what is being said.

7.     Don't worry about the exact next question you're going to ask instead pay attention to the types of questions your asking.

*Inquiry – a seeking or request for truth, information, or knowledge [Origin: 1400–50; ME enquery]*

Here are five types of questions, used in the following sequence, that will help uncover what you need to know about a prospective client and determine how or if you can be of value to them.

## Background Questions

The goal of background questions is to gain an understanding of who the client is and the life around them. Background questions are relatively non-invasive and a good place to start. Here are some examples:

Tell me a little about yourself and your family, if you would.

Where are you from originally?

What do you do for a living?

What do you enjoy doing when you're not working?

What is your risk tolerance?

## Goal Questions

Goal questions help to reveal what's really important to clients and what they value. These are a little more personal but exciting to talk about. Here are some examples:

### Financial Goals

What are your financial goals?

How do you determine the success of an investment?

### Life Goals

What's important to you?

Who in your life do you care about most?

What are three goals you have yet to accomplish in your life?

If you didn't have to work anymore, what would you do?

### Retirement Goals

When do you want to retire?

What is your picture of an ideal retirement?

How much money would need to not worry about money?

### Legacy Goals

What are your legacy goals?

How do you want people to remember you?

How do you measure a person's success in life?

What goals do you have for your loved ones?

*It's not the question, but the type of question that matters. Don't worry about the next "exact question" you're going to ask instead be aware of the type of question you need to ask. Have you asked enough **background** questions to have an understanding of who they are? Have you asked enough **goal** questions to know what really important to them and to understand their picture of an ideal life? Have you asked enough **gap** questions to understand their current financial picture and habits and reveal the barriers keeping them from realizing their financial and life goals? Have you asked enough **affect** questions to determine if the ramifications associated with the barriers are of concern to them?*

*Have you asked enough questions to know what their core resonant needs are?*

## Gap Questions

Gap questions are designed to reveal the issues keeping someone from best realizing their financial, life, retirement and legacy goals? These are far more intimate questions that focus on a client's current financial picture and habits. Here are some examples:

What is your current financial picture? Income, outflow, retirement savings, cash, portfolio, debt, insurance?

Do you have a formal financial plan in place?

What are you not getting from your financial advisor?

On a scale from 0 to 10, how much confidence do you have in your financial plan?

What do you think may happen to your financial picture over the next year, over the next five years?

What would you like to be doing better financially?

What's getting in the way of optimizing your wealth?

What are your key concerns about realizing your goals?

## Affect Questions

Seemingly obvious questions at times, affect questions are designed to highlight the ramifications of a barrier, issue or opportunity. They help you determine if an issue really is an issue to a client. Here are some examples:

How does the barrier, issue or opportunity affect your investment returns?

How does the barrier, issue or opportunity affect you and your family?

How does the barrier, issue or opportunity affect your life and legacy?

How does the barrier, issue or opportunity affect your ability to realize your financial goals?

How does the barrier, issue or opportunity affect your piece of mind?

## Core Resonant Need Questions

Core resonant need questions are designed to reveal the clients ultimate need, the need they value the most that you can help fulfill. This can also be a statement with an affirmation question.

With all this said what do you think you ultimately need to best realize your goals?

Based on what you shared with me it seems what you need most is... do I have that right?

### Levels of Intimacy

Ultimately getting people to reveal the kind of intimate information you need to do your job effectively requires real tact. You want prospective clients, people who don't really know you, to open up and tell you things that they don't normally share with others. If you become too personal without permission, or without a purpose, most people will reveal very little. So it's important to move graciously from one level of intimacy to the next, to start off unobtrusively and then slowly get closer and more intimate as the questions and the answers become more personal.

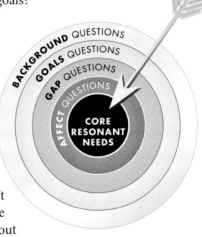

## THE BRIDGE TO THE STRATEGY PRESENTATION

The purpose of the bridge between inquiry and the presentation of the strategy is to act upon what you said in the first bridge – *in order to know how I can help you I need to ask some questions* – and to reinforce that the information the client revealed to you is the basis for the strategy you've developed. It also, like all the bridges, seeks explicit approval to move forward. An effective bridge between inquiry and plan presentation could sound something like this.

"Based on what you shared with me I've developed an effective strategy (financial plan) that will help you overcome [fill in barrier or issue] and best realize your [fill in goals]. May I share it with you?"

## THE VALUE-CENTRIC PRESENTATION

Once you've gained a good understanding of the client their goals, and have an intimate understanding of their life and financial situation, the next step in the advisory process is to craft an effective financial strategy. Then present the strategy so that the client fully understands it and can make a highly informed decision about it. To do this and to help clients feel confident about making their decision you want to communicate; 1– the reasoning behind the strategy; 2– the value it brings, and; 3– how to put the strategy into action. Here's an example of the core components of a value-centric presentation.

### ▲ Introduction

The bridge serves as your introduction and again reinforces that the strategy is customized and based on the information they revealed to you in the previous meeting.

"Based on what you shared with me I've developed some strategies (financial plan) that will help you overcome [fill in barrier or issue] and best realize your [fill in goals]. May I share them with you?"

### ▲ Agenda

"What I'd like to do is talk first about our analysis of your current financial picture based what you told us the last time we met, next I want to tell how we think we can help, and finally, if it makes sense how we can put it into action. Does that sound ok to you?"

## ▲ Analysis of Current Financial Picture

In this topic you want to walk through the information the client shared with you to reaffirm what you heard, articulate the gaps or opportunities you uncovered in your analysis and ultimately create some level of distress or desire with the client. If the discussion doesn't create distress or desire, if it doesn't envoke a need to do something, then there's really no point in continuing. Just as in the inquiry process, tact is important in discussing and analyzing their personal lives during the presentation. Here are some key bullet points for this topic.

▲ Their Goals – what's important to them?

▲ Their Current Financial Picture/Plan – where are they now?

▲ The Gaps or Opportunities – what's in their way?

▲ Their Affect – what does it mean?

▲ Their Core Resonant Needs – what do they ultimately need?

The goal of this topic is to help prospective clients realize there is an issue that needs to be addressed or that there is an opportunity to take advantage of and that there are significant ramifications associated with each. Once you've done this you can move on to the next topic and talk about what you can do to help clients address the barriers or issues that are keeping them from best realizing their financial and life goals.

## ▲ How we can help

This part of the presentation is all about value. It's about the value of your strategy in helping clients overcome the barriers, and resolve the issues, that are keeping them from optimizing their wealth. This topic is about the value attributes (Practice 2) that fill the gaps between what clients are doing and what clients need to do to best realize their life and legacy goals. In this topic you want to tie the value attributes and the gaps (absence of doing the optimal things) together, showing how the attributes remove the barriers or resolve the issues that keep clients from optimizing their wealth. Lastly you want to connect the improved optimization of their wealth to their life and legacy goals. An example or story can be useful here to help the prospect visualize the outcome. Here are some key bullet points for this topic.

▲ What you can do to help them – your value attributes

▲ What the strategy will do for them – remove barriers to optimizing wealth

▲ What it will ultimately mean to them – the affect on their life and legacy goals

▲ A story to help visualize the value and outcome of the strategy

The goal of Topic 2 is to help prospective clients gain a firm grasp and a real appreciation of what you can do for them. This is where the real buy-in occurs and once this happens you can move on to the last topic.

▲ **Putting it in to action**

The last part of the presentation is about the nuts and bolts of executing the strategy. It explains the products and services that deliver the strategy's value attributes while revealing all costs and expenses. The goal of this topic is to clearly explain the actions needed to implement the strategy, and link the products and their value to what they do to help the prospect optimize their wealth and best realize their ideal life and legacy. This is also the time to talk about the administrative process for becoming a client.

▲ Products that drive strategy – describe using value sandwich

▲ Proposed outcome from strategy

▲ Process for becoming a client

By the end of this topic and the body of the presentation the prospective client should have a clear of understanding of the reasoning behind the plan, the value the plan delivers and how it's implemented, leaving them ready to, and capable of, making a highly informed decision.

# GAINING COMMITMENT

Now it's time to ask the prospect if they're ready to move forward. If you've created a strong connection with the help of a meaningful introduction, done a great job of getting to the truth through effective inquiry, crafted an effective strategy and presented it so that your prospect really gets it – how it works and the value of it – there is a good chance they'll say yes. But of course this isn't always the case. Prospects do say no and for a variety of reasons, some are internal – like fear or uncertainty about war or the economy, simple procrastination or even a hidden agenda – and some are external – circumstances have changed in their personal lives or financial picture since you last met.

The process for resolving the issue or concern starts with finding out what the issue is and asking the questions, "What has changed?" What is keeping you from moving forward?" You'll find out what the issue is and be able to determine if it is an internal or external reason. If it's **internal**; they're unable to make a decision because of all that's going on in the world around them or maybe there's something that they really want but haven't articulated you can take the following steps to try to resolve the issue and help them move forward.

1. Have them talk about their concerns – listen, reflect on and validate their concerns.

2. Search for the root cause of the concern, the underlying problems and issues.

3. Have the prospect talk about the issue, the problem and how it's affecting them.

4. Create options, what are some alternatives to addressing the underlying needs that still exist.

5. Determine what the best option is.

If it's an **external** issue and circumstances have changed in their lives you can just use steps 3 – 5 from above.

1. Have the prospect talk about the issue, what's the problem and how is it affecting them.

2. Create options, what are some alternatives to addressing the underlying needs that still exist.

3. Determine what the best option is.

The goal of the advisory process is to help people make informed decisions that will help them optimize their wealth and realize their ideal life. A critical step in this process is resolving the fear, uncertainty, procrastination or issues keeping them from moving forward.

## BEING A TRUE ADVISOR

Your ultimate success with the advisory process is based on the mastery of Practices 1 through 6 – there are no shortcuts. You can't be a *true advisor* unless your focus, objective, expertise, deliverables, communication and process are aligned with what consumers want and need. If you try to just change your process without realigning the other attributes it'll be a little like a wolf in sheep's clothing. It may look like a sheep at first glance but once you get close you can tell what's really underneath.

The consultative client-focused advisory process is the essence of what the best consistently do to engage prospective clients and if appropriate, bring them on board as clients. The client-focused advisory process isn't an isolated event but instead an ongoing conversation - to track progress, to express fears or concerns, to reaffirm goals and life situation, and to adjust plans if needed. It's the path to building meaningful intimate relationships and developing clients for life.

## THE LAST WORD

The affluent market – from the mass affluent to the very affluent – offers an unprecedented opportunity for financial advisors that fulfill the role of true advisor. Consumers, ever wary of salespeople with a product pitch, are looking for financial advisors that have their clients' best interests at heart and the capacity to help their clients realize their important and intimate financial and life goals. The purpose of this book is to help you be that kind of advisor and as a result build a more successful, sustainable and compliant advisory practice. So wherever you are on the value continuum, use *The Seven Practices* to align what you do with what the affluent market is looking for and commit to integrating the perspectives, knowledge, language and processes proven to attract the more affluent consumer and drive top producer results.

Ultimately embracing a more client-focused business model and fulfilling the role of true advisor will help you lead a life of greater significance and relevance – producing the good life for you and those you serve.

**Practice 6 – Convey Real Value**

True advisors are able to effectively convey their value through what they say, do and are. Note some examples of how you convey your value?

Craft your own purpose statement. A concise meaningful description of what you do, of the value you offer.

Describe how you deliver the value you offer and how you work with clients.

Using the value sandwich concept to describe three of the products you use.

How can you change your collateral material (brochures, websites, etc.), the seminars you conduct, and other promotional activities to better convey your value?

What can you change or do more of to enhance your presence?

**Practice 7– Employ a Consultative Client-Focused Approach**

What are the purpose and key components of a meaningful introduction?

Craft a meaningful introduction.

What are the purpose and key components of the bridge between the introduction and inquiry?

Craft a bridge to transition from your meaningful introduction to inquiry.

What are the six basic principles for effective inquiry?

What are the five types of questions that reveal the truth about a prospect?

What is the ideal order to ask them?

Why?

What are the purpose and key components of the bridge between effective inquiry and strategy presentation?

What is the purpose of a value-centric strategy presentation?

Craft a bridge to transition from inquiry to strategy presentation.

What are the three key topics and bullet points in a value-centric presentation?

What two types of barriers can keep a prospect from moving forward?

What steps can you take to overcome each?

# My Plan For Being A True Advisor

# Thomas F. Rieman

Tom Rieman is founder of Impact Training and Consulting, Inc., a firm dedicated to developing best-in-industry financial services professionals. Known as a pioneer in his efforts, Tom helps the best become even better and maintains a reputation in the financial services industry for getting results. *The Seven Practices* are the cornerstone of Tom's consulting work with a client list that includes MetLife, Manulife Financial, John Hancock, Phoenix Home Life, Prudential Financial and Lincoln Financial Group.

Tom's sales, marketing and consulting career spans three decades in the Fortune 500 marketplace with fifteen of those years dedicated to the financial services industry. He has an intimate understanding of the financial services industry at the wholesale and retail level and from the field to the boardroom. Tom is also recognized as an influential speaker with a true ability to inspire and motivate while his classroom facilitation skills are well honed and receive continuous praise.

What helps Tom stand apart is his passion for understanding the complexities of the world. While always having a deep interest in the sciences, Tom's perspectives go well beyond the financial services industry and are greatly influenced by the experiences gained through his graduate studies in Organizational Learning. While firmly rooted in the realities of the financial services professional Tom leverages well-grounded principles and perspectives from numerous disciplines in the pursuit of organizational innovation and excellence.

Tom holds a MS in Organizational Learning from George Mason University and a BA in Marketing from Florida Atlantic University. A native Floridian, he now resides with his wife in Texas.

# Robert L. Schein

Robert L. Schein is partner of The Blanke Schein Group and Vice President with Morgan Stanley in Palm Desert, California. Selected as REUTERS ADVICEPOINT TOP ADVISOR for 2008, Robert is one of Morgan Stanley's youngest to hold the title of WEALTH ADVISOR – a group of their top 1,000 high net worth advisors. He also attended Wharton Business School where he acquired INVESTMENT CONSULTANT designation. The Blanke Schein Group manages over $400 million and $10 million per year in insurance premium.

Mr. Schein is an active force in his community, he serves on the Executive Board for the Family YMCA, works with The College of the Desert as Chairman of the Planned Gift Committee and sits on the Board of Director's for Xavier College Preparatory High School.

Robert received degrees in Finance and Marketing at The University of Arizona and resides in Indio, California, with his wife and three children.

# SUGGESTED ADDITIONAL READING

## SECTION ONE

*The Quest for Resilience,* Harvard Business Review, September 2003, Gary Hamel and Liisa Valikangas

*Competing for the Future,* Harvard Business Press, 1994, Gary Hamel and C.K. Prahalad

*The Future of Competition, Co Creating Unique Value at the Consumer Level,* Harvard Business Press, 2004, C.K. Prahalad and Venkat Ramaswamy

*What Got You Here Won't Get You There: How Successful People Become Even More Successful,* Hyperion Publishing, 2007, Marshall Goldsmith and Mark Reiter

*Overcoming Organizational Defenses,* Allyn and Bacon, 1990, Chris Argyris

*Million Dollar Consulting,* McGraw Hill, 2003, Alan Weiss

## SECTION TWO

*Jesus – CEO: Using Ancient Wisdom for Visionary Leadership,* Hyperion, 1995, Laurie Beth Jones

## SECTION THREE

*Leadership and the New Science,* Berrett-Koehler, 1999, Margaret Wheatley

*Becoming a Strategic Thinker on a Daily Basis,* Centre for Strategic Management®, 2006, Stephan Haines, available at: www.hainescentre.com/essence/pdfs/abst.pdf,

SECTION FOUR

*Birth of a Chaordic Age,* Berret Koelher, 1999, Dee Hock

*Consilience: The Unity of Knowledge,* Vintage Books, 1998,
Edward O. Wilson

*Dancing Wu-Li Masters: An Overview of the New Physics,*
Perennial Classics, 1979, Gary Zukav

*The Social Life of Information,* Harvard Business School Press,
2002, John Seely Brown and Paul Duguid

*The Balanced Scorecard: Translating Strategy into Action,*
Harvard Business Press, 1996, Robert S. Kaplan and David P. Norton

SECTION FIVE

*Flawless Consulting: A Guide to Getting Your Expertise Used,*
Pfeiffer & Company, 1981, Peter Block

## REFERENCES

CHAPTER ONE

1. 2006 McKinsey and Company Report, *The Retirement Journey: Pathways to Success in the New Retirement Market*

2. 2005 CEG Worldwide, Derived from *All the Right Moves, The Best Practices of Today's Top Independent Broker-Dealer Representatives*

3. 2008 Cogent Research, Source article, Investment News, April 30, 2008, *Clients are Seeing Other Advisors*

4. 2008 Phoenix Companies, *Avoid Commoditization: Become a Risk Manager,* Source article, Investment News, July 1, 2008, *Moving Past Pessimism with a Bullish Outlook*

5. *The Quest for Resilance,* Harvard Business Review, September 1, 2003, Gary Hamel and Liisa Valikangas

CHAPTER TWO

1. 2006 McKinsey and Company Report, *The Retirement Journey: Pathways to Success in the New Retirement Market*

CHAPTER THREE

1. The effectiveness of client-focused business models in creating loyal repeat customers is evident in the success of companies like the Ritz Carlton, The Four Seasons and Virgin Atlantic Airways.

2. *Wealth management* definition from Wikipedia

3. 2008 Phoenix Companies, *Avoid Commoditization: Become a Risk Manager,* Source article, Investment News, July 1, 2008, *Moving Past Pessimism with a Bullish Outlook*

4. Case Western University, 2006, Derived from *Investment Consumer Satisfaction: Defining Loyalty in Financial Advisory Relationships,* Betty Moon, Executive Doctor of Management Program

CHAPTER FIVE

1. Product descriptions derived from information found at www.sec.gov.answers, www.finra.org and www.mfea.com

CHAPTER SEVEN

1. *How to Build Your Total Brand,* BuildingBrands, Ltd, 2004, Colin Bates

# INDEX

## A

affect questions, 164
affluent clients, 12, 15, 21, 26, 30, 31, 38, 40, 49, 50, 62, 96, 108, 124, 126, 145, 147, 154, 155
affluent consumer, 12, 29, 108, 146, 147, 170
affluent consumers, 12, 20, 21, 26, 28, 51, 119, 137, 138
alternative investments, 94, 95, 113
annuity fees and expenses, 73

## B

background question, 162, 164
best in the industry, 14, 20, 31, 32, 35, 36, 48, 56, 144, 145, 156
brand, 122, 123, 124, 127, 131, 136, 138, 154, 158
branding, 15, 32, 35, 118, 119, 122, 126, 132
bridge, 160, 161, 166, 173, 174
bridges, 159, 166
broker dealer, 15
business case, 14, 20

## C

C.K. Prahalad, 24
Case Western University, 54
CEG Worldwide, 23
Chaos Theory, 120
client first strategy, 14, 55
client-focused advisor attributes, 56, 98, 119, 146, 156
client-focused advisors, 24, 156
client-focused advisory process, 15, 155, 156, 158
client-focused business model, 12, 14, 20, 30, 57, 131
client-focused language, 48, 58, 63
client-focused seminar, 149
client-focused strategy, 14, 48, 68, 119, 145, 147
Cogent Research, 26
Colin Bates, 122
commoditized, 26, 27, 129
communicate, 22, 35, 36, 58, 62, 63, 70, 125, 145, 146, 154, 166, 168
communication, 130, 145, 146, 170
competitive convergence, 13, 21, 26
comprehensive and consultative services, 12, 18, 27, 29
comprehensive services, 14, 22, 30, 31, 33, 35, 68, 69, 96, 98, 108, 109, 147, 152, 158, 170
congruence, 125
consultative approach, 14, 30, 31, 33, 147, 148, 149, 170
consultative advisory process, 15, 144, 156, 158
consumer needs, 13, 21, 109
convey real value, 15, 144
convey value, 144, 145, 146, 155, 160

*Bridging the Value Gap*

## W

wealth management, 51, 64
wealth Optimization, 4, 52, 53, 64, 108, 120, 134, 154, 158, 170
wealth optimization strategies, 98, 108, 115, 120, 131
wealth optimization strategy development, 98, 101
wholesaler, 18, 25, 70, 129
wholesalers, 4, 15, 25, 32, 38, 45, 96, 124, 128, 129, 130, 140
worldview, 59, 146

## Z

zealous intent, 37, 44

IMPACT
TRAINING & CONSULTING

Impact helps financial advisors, and the wholesalers that support them, become true advisors and build more successful and sustainable practices.

For more information on Impact's services, keynote presentations, workshops and other available resources, please visit.

www.thesevenpractices.com

or call: 888.479.9623

TOM RIEMAN
Author / Founder
Impact Training & Consulting

# The Seven Practices of High-Value Financial Services Professionals™

## Embrace a Client-Focused Strategy

PRACTICE 1
Be Driven to Help Others Succeed

PRACTICE 2
Have a Deep Understanding of the Value You Offer

## Offer Comprehensive Services

PRACTICE 3
Have In-Depth Knowledge of Financial Planning

PRACTICE 4
Develop Highly Effective Strategies

## Maximize Your Market Impact

PRACTICE 5
Utilize High Performance Business Processes

## Be a True Advisor

PRACTICE 6
Effectively Convey Value

PRACTICE 7
Employ a Consultative Client-Focused Approach